THE COMPLEAT TRAVELER'S COMPANION

TENNESSEE

A Guide to the Volunteer State

by

GEORGE SCHEER III

BURT FRANKLIN & CO.

Published by Burt Franklin & Company, Inc.
235 East Forty-fourth Street
New York, New York 10017

Library of Congress Cataloging in Publication Data
Scheer, George.
Tennessee, a guide to the Volunteer State.
(The Compleat traveler's companion)
1.   Tennessee—Description and travel—1981   —Guide-books.
2.   Historic sites—Tennessee—Guide-books.
I.   Title.   II.   Series
F434.3.S33   917.68'0453   82-2547
ISBN 0-89102-262-7 (pbk.)   AACR2

3 4 2

Manufactured in the United States of America

CONTENTS

ACKNOWLEDGMENTS

A book of this nature is perforce the work of many hands; so it pleases me to acknowledge the assistance of scores of curators, administrators, and organizations for their hospitality and for their patient responses to my detailed queries. Their very number precludes my thanking each by name, but I trust they will be aware of my gratitude and indebtedness. I cannot, however, forgo special thanks to the Tennessee Department of Tourist Development, which furnished many of the photographs in this volume. I would particularly like to thank Don Wick, of that office, who generously shared his vast knowledge of Tennessee, cheerfully undertook to read the complete manuscript, and made a number of valuable suggestions. His cooperation and encouragement helped to make the preparation of this book a pleasant task.

GEORGE SCHEER III

Chapel Hill, North Carolina

INTRODUCTION

It was on the Appalachian frontier that Americans first displayed the qualities that were forever to distinguish them from their European forebears. On that frontier, Tennessee, unlike its neighbors on the Atlantic seaboard, was settled by Americans, men once removed from Europe's old ways. They treasured America for its freedom, its opportunity, and its abundance, and they hungered for more of each than the Eastern Seaboard could offer; so, to fulfill the promise that had drawn ships over the sea to Roanoke Island and Jamestown, they came over the mountains to the wilderness that was to become Tennessee. Life in the coastal colonies whence they came imitated European society, but on the Appalachian frontier they struck their life from a new mold. The early history of Tennessee is peopled with figures—Daniel Boone, John Sevier, Davy Crockett, Sam Houston, Andrew Jackson—who became models for an America in search of frontiers. They were bold, adventurous, independent, resourceful, and charismatic; occasionally they were arrogant, avaricious, and ruthless as well.

Although their exploits have become the stuff of legend, these men were real. And their mark is on the land in Tennessee. You will see it at Cumberland Gap, where, in 1775, Daniel Boone blazed the Wilderness Road through the blue-green wall of the Cumberland Mountains into Tennessee and "Kaintuck"; at Sycamore Shoals on the Watauga River, where

John Sevier and Issac Shelby rallied the Overmountain Men for the march to their decisive victory over a Tory army at the Revolution's battle of Kings Mountain in 1780; at Limestone, where Davy Crockett was born in a cabin on the banks of the Nolichucky River in 1786; at the one-room log schoolhouse near Maryville where Sam Houston found his calling as a schoolmaster; at Jonesboro, Tennessee's oldest town, where Andrew Jackson was admitted to the bar in 1788.

Neither is the common man forgotten in Tennessee. At Norris, the Museum of Appalachia is a complete frontier village, where more than thirty reconstructed and fully furnished log houses create a complete vision of day-to-day life on the Appalachian frontier. At Cades Cove in the Great Smoky Mountains National Park, split-rail fences and log cabins have been preserved from the homesteads that once dotted the valley. And numerous shops and festivals keep alive the cherished crafts and folkways of the resourceful pioneers. At Chickamauga-Chattanooga, Stones River, and Shiloh the terrible days of the Civil War are remembered. In the twentieth century, every American life has been changed by the atomic research pursued in the once secret town of Oak Ridge, where today the American Museum of Science and Energy reveals its meaning for us all. And those fortunate enough to visit Tennessee during the summer of 1982 will find at Knoxville the 1982 World's Fair, the first official world's fair to be held since 1975 and the first fair sanctioned by the Bureau of International Expositions in Paris ever to be held in the southeastern United States.

Tennessee has bred its own distinctive music, its own gaited horses, and its own sipping whiskey. From Memphis, where the blues flourished on immortal Beale Street and Elvis Presley gave birth to rock 'n' roll at the Sun recording studios, to Nashville, where the "Grand Ole Opry" has been an American Saturday-night institution for more than half a

An architect's model of the 70-acre site for the World's Fair scheduled for May 1 through October 31, 1982, in Knoxville. A 1,200-foot-long lake has been created for the fair in the heart of Knoxville. Architecrural highlights include the Sunsphere, the theme structure at center; the Tennessee State Amphitheatre, a tension-fabric structure near the base of the Sunsphere; the solar-powered United States Pavilion on the southern lakeshore at right; and the restored L & N Railway Depot at upper left, one of twelve historic structures incorporated into the World's Fair site.

century, the visitor can see fascinating landmarks of American popular music. In the rolling bluegrass pasturelands of Middle Tennessee, around Shelbyville, Tennessee walking horses are bred and trained. At the small town of Lynchburg, the Jack Daniel Distillery is the oldest registered whiskey-maker in the United States.

Everywhere Tennessee is a land of gentle beauty and vitality, from the breathtaking sweep of the Great Smoky Mountains, through the wooded hills of Middle Tennessee, to the broad vistas along the mighty Mississippi River in the west. More than half of the state remains forested, and much of its most beautiful land is preserved for public use; from any point in Tennessee a state park is within an hour's drive.

A model of the Sunsphere, the theme structure for the 1982 World's Fair at Knoxville.

HOW TO USE THIS BOOK

In this guide to Tennessee's riches, the reader will find attractions appealing to a breadth of interests. Although historic and cultural sites are emphasized, I recognize that even the most studious museum-goer, history buff, or old-house enthusiast will occasionally want to see something more of our times—and the visitor may be traveling with family members or companions who seek something livelier than Civil War earthworks. So here you will find a wide variety of things to see and do.

Tennessee appears in relief to be a gradually subsiding series of ripples, from the 6,000-foot peaks of the Appalachians in the east, through the lesser ridges and plateaus in the state's midlands, to the virtually flat alluvial bottomlands of the Mississippi Valley in the west. From this continuum, its three distinct regions emerge, the character of each shaped by the nature of its land and the circumstances of its settlement. Each of these three regions, recognized as "Grand Divisions" by the state constitution, is treated in a separate section of this guide.

> *East Tennessee* is mountain country from the Unaka Mountains westward to the sharp escarpment of the Cumberland Plateau, called by early setters the "Wilderness" for its imposing and barren nature, with the great valley of East Tennessee between.

From wood carving to hand-thrown pottery, traditional craft skills endure in Tennessee, encouraged by dozens of arts-and-crafts shows held each year throughout the state.

Middle Tennessee, from the eastern edge of the Cumberland Plateau westward to the second passage of the Tennessee River, is a land of rolling hills where fertile limestone soil supports crops and lush bluegrass pasturage.

West Tennessee shares as much with the Deep South as it does with the balance of its own state. Much of its land is reminiscent of the Mississippi Delta, sloping gradually away from the modest heights near the Tennessee River into low, flat terrain as it approaches the banks of the Mississippi. Although early settlement was occasionally impeded by rugged hills, dense swamps, and frequent flooding in the bottomlands, the deep, fertile alluvial land encouraged the cultivation of cotton and the creation of large plantations.

In each of these three sections of the guide, each site is to be found under its geographic location, usually a town, occasionally a national park, national forest, or scenic highway, and the locations are arranged alphabetically.

This guide can best be enjoyed by acquiring and referring to the official state highway map; using the map in conjunction with a sketch map herein, the traveler can readily determine which towns lie within the compass of his projected travel. Reference to the descriptions of specific towns in this volume will suggest things to see and do.

The visiting hours given here are as up-to-date as possible, but funds fluctuate and operating schedules change, though usually only the opening and closing times. If you plan to visit at a marginal time and cannot bear to be disappointed, call ahead. I have provided the telephone numbers whenever possible.

Fees

Admission fees change more frequently—and more predictably. I have categorized admission charges in three ways: "Free;" "Nominal charge," $2 or less for adults; and "Fee charged," more than $2 for adults. Most sites charge less for children; many admit young children free; some offer senior citizens' discounts (which are indicated). The Golden Age Passport, free to any senior (over sixty-two years) upon presentation in person of proof of age at any National Park Service area that charges an entrance fee, any National Park Service regional office, or National Park Service Headquarters, Room 1013, U.S. Department of the Interior, Eighteenth and C streets, NW, Washington, DC 20240, admits the bearer free to all national parks and National Park Service historic sites; it also entitles the bearer and his family to a 50 percent discount on recreational-use fees. Any traveler planing to visit several national parks, forests, or recreation areas should consider purchasing, for $10, a Golden Eagle Pass, which for a full year admits the holder and his party to all such areas where an entrance fee is charged.

For further information

The Tennessee traveler should consult, in addition to this volume, several readily available sources of information.

Department of Tourist Development,

State of Tennessee,
P.O. Box 23170,
Nashville, TN 37202.
615-741-2158.

This is the principal source of travel and background information. Its publications include booklets on camping areas, golf courses, state symbols and facts, historic sites, state parks, fall-winter and spring-summer calendars of events, and a guide to outdoor recreation that includes information on river running, hunting, hang-gliding, diving, hiking, and even houseboat rentals. Be certain to request a state map also.

Northwest Tennessee Tourism Association,
  P.O. Box 63,
  Martin, TN 38237.
  901-587-4215.
Southwest Tourism Organization,
  P.O. Box 1925,
  Jackson, TN 38301.
  901-423-0722.
South Central Tourism Organization,
  245 E. Gaines Street,
  Lawrenceburg, TN 38464.
  615-762-6944.
Upper Cumberland Tourist Association,
  P.O. Box 698,
  Cookeville, TN 38501.
  615-526-7100.
Upper East Tennessee–Southwest Virginia
  Tourism Council,
  P.O. Box 375,
  Jonesboro, TN 37659.
  615-753-5961.

The regional tourist offices are additional sources of information about attractions in their respective geographic areas. The travel offices of the major cities will also have information about their surrounding areas.

Information Office,
  Tennessee Department of Transportation,
  105-A Highway Building,
  Nashville, TN 37219.
  615-741-2848.

The Department of Transportation will provide on request the official state highway map.

Tennessee Historical Commission,
4721 Trousdale Drive,
Nashville, TN 37203.
615-741-2371.

Although the commission itself does not manage historic sites, it can provide information.

Tennessee Arts Commission,
222 Capitol Hill Building,
Nashville, TN 37219.
615-741-1701.

Most of the major museums and art events are described in the literature of the Tourist Development office, but questions specifically about the arts can be directed to the information office of the Arts Commission.

Association for the Preservation of Tennessee Antiquities,
Belle Meade Mansion,
110 Leake Avenue,
Nashville, TN 37205.
615-352-7350.

The Association for the Preservation of Tennessee Antiquities (APTA) maintains fourteen historic properties throughout Tennessee, ranging in period from a frontier station and a pioneer log cabin, through handsome antebellum plantation manors, to elegant homes of the Victorian era. Most have been restored with period furnishings. Individual admissions are charged. The APTA publishes a brochure with a brief description and a picture of each and a map showing their locations.

Tennessee State Parks Division,
2611 West End Avenue.
Nashville, TN 37203.
615-741-3251.

The nearly forty Tennessee state parks offer diverse recreational opportunities, are classified by primary emphasis—resort, natural rustic, historical, scenic river, day use, archaeological, environmental education—and have appropriate facilities in each category. The resort parks are the most fully developed, with inns, restaurants, golf courses, tennis courts, and other leisure facilities, but almost all the parks have playgrounds, picnic sites, nature trails, boating and fishing facilities, and campsites. Some rustic parks have vacation cabins, and some of the historical and archaeological parks have interpretative programs and museums. Folklore programs featuring traditional crafts, skills, and music are mounted at selected parks each summer. Individual park brochures and lodging information, as well as a guide to the entire park system, are available on request.

Tennessee Wildlife Resources Agency,
  P.O. Box 40747,
  Nashville, TN 37204.
  615-741-1512.
Tennessee boasts more than half a million acres of fishing waters, with quarry ranging from wary 8-inch brook trout high in the eastern mountains to 100-pound blue catfish in the murky Mississippi River. Write or phone the agency for detailed information on fishing and hunting or to purchase a license by mail.

Tennessee Valley Authority,
  Information Office,
  Knoxville, TN 37902.
  615-632-2101.
Twenty-one TVA impoundments have shoreline in Tennessee, and several more are in adjacent states. Many are surrounded by developed recreation areas, including state and local parks. "Recreation on TVA Lakes," a map showing the

More than thirty rivers and streams offer a wide variety of scenic canoeing waters in Tennessee. Typically the eastern rivers offer fast runs on challenging white water, while the gentler rivers in Middle and West Tennessee offer miles of peaceful boating and fishing waters.

During the spring and summer, pickin' and fiddlin' festivals blossom across Tennessee like the dogwood and rhododendron.

entire TVA system with a listing of recreational areas and their facilities, is available by request from the Information Office. Maps of each individual lake, showing detailed routes to shoreline recreation areas, are also free. Navigational charts of TVA waters may be purchased from: TVA Maps, Knoxville, TN 37902, or Chattanooga, TN 37401. The Information Office also distributes a series of brochures on various canoeing rivers and streams, with difficulty ratings, access points, and stream-flow information. A separate brochure lists commercial canoe- and raft-rental services. For up-to-date stream-flow readings call 615-525-5751.

U.S. Army Engineer District Office,
P.O. Box 1070,
Nashville, TN 37202.
615-251-7161.

Seven Tennessee lakes created and maintained by the Army Corps of Engineers have been developed for public recreation. All offer developed and primitive campsites, a visitors' center, tours of the dams, interpretative programs, and a wide range of aquatic recreational facilities. Maps and detailed descriptions are available from the Nashville office.

National Cave Association,
Route 9, Box 106,
McMinnville, TN 37110.
615-668-3925.

Over millions of years, underground streams have carved thousands of caverns in the limestone of Middle and East Tennessee. More than two thousand have been discovered, and the full extent of some cave systems has yet to be explored. A number are open to the public commercially year-round; of those that close in winter, some will accommodate group tours or welcome spelunking expeditions led by qualified guides. The fully developed commercial caves offer the thrill of exploring fascinating geological phenomena from the comfort and safety of well-lit, gently graded pathways—ideal for those who abide by the National Cave Association's dictum that anyone who confuses stalactites with stalagmites should never go underground without a guide. Additional information, including a list of commercial caves, is available from the Tennessee Tourist Development Office.

THE "GREAT STATE OF TENNESSEE"

When in 1541 the conquistador Hernando de Soto, the first white man to enter the region, raised a Spanish flag on a bluff near present-day Memphis, western Tennessee was the domain of the Chickasaw Indians. Gone were the earlier Indians of the Archaic, the Woodland, and the Mississippian periods, as well as the Stone Age Paleo-Indians, having left an intriguing record of their presence in such edifices as the Pinson Mounds near present-day Jackson. De Soto, wealthy with riches he had plundered from the Inca when he had accompanied Francisco Pizarro in the conquest of Peru, was insatiably ambitious and envisioned for himself a viceroyalty in the northern American hemisphere to rival those of Mexico and Peru. With a private army of some five hundred men, brought to Florida in his private fleet of seventeen ships, he began in 1539 what was to become a toilsome four-year trek into the southeastern North American interior in search of empire. Two years after his pause at Memphis, he was dead of fever, his corpse disposed of in the Mississippi River to keep it out of the hands of the Indians. He had failed, but his invasion of the lands of the Tennessee Indians marked the beginning of the white man's encroachment in what was to become the "great state of Tennessee."

More than a century passed, however, before the next white men came, simultaneously from the east and the west. On their voyage of discovery down the Mississippi from Canada in 1673, two Frenchmen—fur trader Louis Joliet and Jesuit missionary Father Jacques Marquette—landed near Memphis, also encountering the Chickasaw. That same year, James Needham and Gabriel Archer, among the first of many "long hunters" and traders from the English settlements in Virginia and Carolina, pushed over the rugged Appalachian wall into what is now East Tennessee and found it inhabited by communities of "Overhill" Cherokee Indians along the Little Tennessee and Tellico rivers.

Although both Spain and France laid claim to the region, Great Britain assumed it was an extension of her North Carolina colony, and the first enduring settlements in Tennessee were English. After the French and Indian War, hundreds and soon thousands of visionary folk of the eastern piedmont crossed the Alleghenies; by the time of the American Revolution there was a constellation of villages in the northeastern corner of what is now Tennessee, by the waters of the Watauga, Nolichucky, and Holston rivers. Feeling they were being ignored by the North Carolina government, these first settlements banded together in 1772 as the Watauga Association, a "homespun" frontier democracy with a constitution called the Watauga Compact—perhaps the first to be adopted by independent Americans—which created a legislature composed of delegates from each tiny village. Under its constitution the association first leased and ultimately bought its lands from the Cherokee.

Upon the outbreak of the Revolution and after their arrangement with the Indians had been violated by an Indian attack and their own counterattack, the Wataugans put themselves under the protection of North Carolina's new independent provincial government. When North Carolina created

Washington County, embracing most of present-day Tennessee, the association went out of existence.

During the Revolution, the white occupation of Tennessee spread farther westward, into the fertile Cumberland Basin of Middle Tennessee. Land speculator Richard Henderson purchased the Indians' tracts that included almost all of today's Kentucky and Middle Tennessee, and in 1779 James Robertson, acting for him, led a group of pioneers through the Cumberland Gap into Kentucky and southward to the French Lick, an old trading post on the Cumberland River, where he established Nashborough (later Nashville). The next spring a second party, led by John Donelson and including his daughter Rachel, the future wife of Andrew Jackson, arrived after a journey of nearly a thousand miles by flatboat down the Tennessee River and up the Ohio and Cumberland rivers. Despite Indian attacks and other "manifold suffering and distresses," the Nashborough settlement survived to become ultimately the capital of Tennessee.

Although some of the tramontane pioneers of East Tennessee joined the fight against the British, Tennessee was not a Revolutionary battleground. But in 1780, when a British major, Patrick Ferguson, leading a Tory force of Lord Cornwallis's invading army, sent word to Colonel Isaac Shelby, whom he considered the titular head of the "backwater men," that if they continued to resist royal authority he would march over the mountains, "hang their leaders, and lay their country waste with fire and sword," the Tennessee "Overmountain Men" did not wait. At Sycamore Shoals on the Watauga River, they rendezvoused under Shelby and Sevier, marched over the mountains, and after gathering up Virginians and South Carolinians along the way, attacked and demolished Ferguson's army at Kings Mountain, on the border between the Carolinas. Ferguson's death in the battle and the defeat of his force temporarily disjointed Cornwallis's plans for an invasion of the upper South and afforded the Continental Army breathing space that was crucial to its ultimate triumph.

North Carolina's constitution of 1776 had provided for eventual statehood for its western lands. Therefore, soon after the war, when North Carolina ceded to the federal government its lands comprising present-day Tennessee, the westerners assembled at Jonesboro and began to draft a state constitution. When, however, North Carolina reneged on its act of cession, the frustrated Tennesseans stubbornly proclaimed themselves the "free state of Franklin" with John Sevier, hero of Kings Mountain, as their governor. For four tempestuous years, as pro- and antiseparatist factions quarreled, the independent state of Franklin survived; with the expiration of Sevier's governorship in 1788, it evaporated, and Sevier was arrested on charges of treason. But he was never tried. After taking an oath of allegiance to North Carolina, he was swiftly elected to that state's senate. With North Carolina's ratification of the federal constitution, the western lands were again ceded to the central government and Tennessee was established as the Southwest Territory. By 1790 East Tennessee had nearly 30,000 inhabitants and the Cumberland settlements in Middle Tennessee somewhat fewer than 10,000. Six years later Tennessee was admitted to the Union as the sixteenth state. Its first governor was John Sevier, who was returned to office five times and dominated its politics during the first two decades of its statehood. Its single seat in the U.S. House of Representatives was filled by young Andrew Jackson, who eventually succeeded Sevier as the preeminent political leader of the new state. Although the state of Franklin had been short-lived, the spirit of independence with which it had been mounted seems to persist in today's proud Tennesseans.

The new state grew rapidly in population. Virginians and North Carolinians, as well as Pennsylvanians and other seaboarders, continued to flow in through the Cumberland Gap, and others came from Kentucky. The fertile lands of the central basin, especially around Nashville, drew settlers, so that ere long more than half the state's population lived in Middle Tennessee. Nashville and Knoxville became thriving frontier towns. On an economy largely of cotton, tobacco, and livestock and to a lesser degree of iron and textile production, the state flourished, sent so many men to fight Great Britain again in the War of 1812 that it earned the sobriquet "Volunteer State," and mounted a campaign that put its greatest hero of that war, Andrew Jackson, into the White House. Before being divided by the Civil War, it became politically strong enough to send two other citizens, James K. Polk and Andrew Johnson, to the presidency.

Although Tennessee seceded from the Union in the summer of 1861 and fortified itself against a Union invasion, in several bloody engagements it was soon overrun, and after the summer of 1862 it lived out the Civil War under the military governorship of Andrew Johnson, who had made Tennessee his home since his youth and had been, along with most East Tennesseans, a strong opponent of secession.

After the war, Tennessee was the first state to re-enter the Union. The majority of Tennesseans returned to their farms, but industrialization grew rapidly, especially in East Tennessee, so that while Memphis in the west became the great cotton center of the South, Knoxville developed coal and iron industries, Chattanooga became a leading steel producer, in Nashville mills to produce wood, paper, and flour sprang up, copper mines opened around Cleveland, and woolen and flour mills opened in Jackson.

The growth of the state was not without its price. By the 1930s the once lovely hill and mountain lands of the Tennessee River Valley had become hopelessly eroded by exploitative farming, and the standard of living throughout the region had become among the lowest in a nation now plunged into stultifying depression. The great river system of the valley drained some forty thousand square miles, principally in Tennessee but also in Virginia, Kentucky, North Carolina, Alabama, Georgia, and Mississippi. Since early in the nineteenth century the valley had been a region subjected to national scrutiny, first for its potential as a major inland channel of transportation and second as a source of waterpower. In 1933 Congress, responding to the urgency of the times, as well as the needs of the valley people, enacted the Tennessee Valley Authority Act, creating an independent agency with enormous powers and responsibilities that included flood control along the 652-mile course of the river, development of its navigational channel, production of electricity, and general concern for the economic and social well-being of the people of the valley. The huge enterprise, involving great and painful dislocations, continues today to be a subject of fierce controversy, although there is little gainsaying that it has wrought an economic and social revolution touching the lives of all Tennesseans by providing electricity at relatively low cost, by averting flood damage that would have cost millions of dollars, by developing some of the country's most spectacular man-made lakes for recreational and tourist activities, and by improving and expanding agriculture and forestry, as well as industry.

EAST TENNESSEE

East Tennessee comprises about one-quarter of the state's land area and includes two of its six major physiographic regions: the Unaka Mountain Range and the great valley of East Tennessee. The Unaka Range is the western side of the Appalachians and includes such mountain groups as the Great Smoky, Bald, and Unicoi mountains, with a dozen or more peaks above six thousand feet. The highest, Clingmans Dome, is at 6,643 feet. Branches of the Tennessee River drain the mountain slopes and divide the region into sharp ridges and deep gorges, and in the past these have separated the people of the region into remote enclaves, isolated from the Eastern Seaboard and from one another. Row-crop farming is impossible in these rugged mountains, and until the advent of tourism, mining and lumbering were the only industries. West of the mountains is the great valley of East Tennessee, part of the ridge-and-valley province of the Appalachian Mountains. Here the erosion of underlying limestone created fertile valleys separated by long, narrow ridges. Coursing through the valley from northeast to southwest is the Tennessee River. Knoxville, Chattanooga, and other cities have made this the most industrialized region of Tennessee.

Opportunities for travelers abound in East Tennessee, whether one seeks the pioneer ambience of Jonesboro, the Civil War battlefields of Chattanooga, or the Atomic Age city

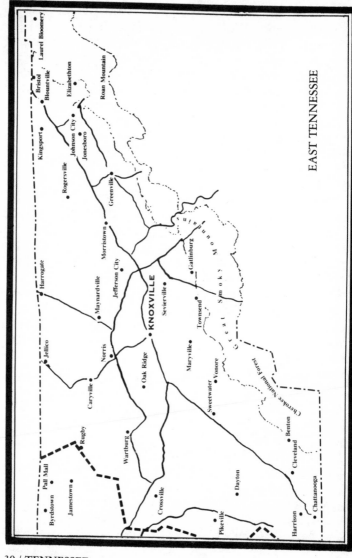

EAST TENNESSEE

Laurel Bloomery
Bristol
Blountville
Elizabethton
Roan Mountain
Kingsport
Johnson City
Jonesboro
Rogersville
Greenville
Morristown
Harrogate
Maynardville
Jefferson City
Gatlinburg
Great Smoky Mountains
KNOXVILLE
Sevierville
Norris
Townsend
Jellico
Caryville
Oak Ridge
Maryville
Vonore
Sweetwater
Cherokee National Forest
Rugby
Wartburg
Benton
Pall Mall
Crossville
Dayton
Cleveland
Byrdstown
Jamestown
Pikeville
Harrison
Chattanooga

of Oak Ridge, where today significant research in nuclear physics and energy development continues. Throughout East Tennessee the beauty of the land is breathtaking, and much of it is preserved in the Great Smoky Mountains National Park and the Cherokee National Forest. In the winter there is skiing, and in the summer numerous outfitters offer guided white-water raft trips. And through the spring, summer, and fall of 1982 the nations of the world will be turning to East Tennessee to exhibit their most advanced technology and their finest cultural treasures at the 1982 World's Fair in Knoxville.

BENTON   *Chilhowee Gliderport,* 5 miles north of Benton on U.S. 411, offers sailplane instruction and services. For a fee, an introductory flight affords a view of the Hiwassee River Valley and the Tennessee Appalachians just to the east. Open daily 11 A.M. until the last person wants to fly. Call ahead in winter. 615-338-2000.

Fort Marr, an original *ca.*-1814 blockhouse that was a supply depot for Andrew Jackson's army in the War of 1812 and later a collection point during the 1838 Cherokee Indian removal from Carolina to Oklahoma, still stands on U.S. 411 in Benton. Free.

BLOUNTVILLE   There are more original log houses along the main street of Blountville than in any other Tennessee town. The *Blountville Historic District,* lying on both sides of Route 126 in the center of town, embraces twenty unaltered eighteenth-century log and nineteenth-century frame and brick homes and public buildings. A walking tour is recommended, and maps are available at the *Anderson Townhouse,* used by Blountville's town commissioners in the late eighteenth century. For information phone 615-323-2431 or 615-246-6635. The *Old Deery Inn* (1794) of log, frame, and stone, with numerous outbuildings, is on Main Street. Al-

Fort Marr, an early-nineteenth-century blockhouse that served as a supply depot during the War of 1812, still stands on U.S. 411 at Benton.

The Anderson Townhouse, used in the late eighteenth century by the first town commissioners of Blountville, where many original log houses survive along Main Street.

though privately owned, it is open during the summer. Tours Mon.–Fri. 10–4. 601-323-5670.

BRISTOL   Brass markers in the middle of State Street designate the boundary line between Virginia and Tennessee, which the town straddles. Here in 1856 the rail lines of the Eastern Seaboard were joined with those of the Mississippi Valley for the first time, when the final spike connected the tracks of the Norfolk and Western to those of the Southern Railway. In the spectacular dripstone caves of *Bristol Caverns,* 5 miles southeast of town on U.S. 421, paved walkways wind through vaulted chambers along an underground river. Open daily 9–7:15 May 15 through September 15; daily 9–5:15 September 16 through May 14. Closed during Sunday church hours. Fee charged. Group rates available. 615-878-2011.

CARYVILLE   *Cove Lake State Day Use Park,* at U.S. 25 and I-75, on the northern edge of the Cumberland Mountains, offers a restaurant, tent and trailer campsites, picnic areas, nature trails, and provisions for fishing, swimming, and boating. Free. Write the park, Caryville, TN 37714. 615-562-8355.

CHATTANOOGA   Chattanooga, on a sweeping bend of the Tennessee River, is surrounded by steep ridges: Signal Mountain to the northwest, Missionary Ridge to the east, and to the southwest, Lookout Mountain, where, a year after Yorktown, an engagement referred to by local historians as the "last battle of the American Revolution" was fought between Chickamauga Indians allied with the British and frontiersmen in the pay of the Continental government.

With direct railroad lines to Nashville and Memphis in the west, Knoxville and ultimately Richmond to the north, and Atlanta and Charleston in the south, Chattanooga became a focus of the Civil War in the west. From the beginning, Union command strategy called for occupation of eastern Tennessee and seizure of the transportation nexus at Chattanooga, which would split the eastern and western armies of the Confederacy and interrupt the flow of their matériel.

A first Union assault failed shortly after Shiloh in 1862, but in the summer of 1863, Major General William Rosecrans approached Confederate-held Chattanooga from the south, intending to sever its sources of supply and compel an evacuation. To avoid ensnarement, Confederate General Braxton Bragg abandoned the city, and the armies maneuvered for advantage. On September 19–20, Bragg flung his army against the Union position at Chickamauga Creek, about 12 miles south of the city in northwest Georgia. They were the two bloodiest days in American military history. More than a quarter of the 124,000 men engaged were killed, wounded, or missing; in some units, casualties exceeded 80 percent. For his staunch resistance to the Confederate assault, Union General George Thomas earned the sobriquet, "Rock of Chickamauga." In a tactical but costly victory, Bragg drove the Union troops into Chattanooga and then initiated a siege, finally broken at the end of November by Union assaults on Lookout Mountain and Missionary Ridge. The "Battle Above the Clouds" raged in a heavy mist on Lookout Mountain until the early morning hours of November 25. That day the last of Bragg's siege lines on Missionary Ridge were broken and he was driven into Georgia. From September 1863 until March 1866, Union forces occupied Chattanooga, where they marshaled support for General Sherman's attack on Atlanta.

Chickamauga and Chattanooga National Military Park contains eight historic areas in some 8,000 acres. A visitors' center at park headquarters, just off U.S. 27, south of Chattanooga, features lectures, demonstrations, and the extensive Fuller collection of military shoulder arms. Historic areas include *Point Park* (see below) on *Lookout Mountain; Orchard Knob* and *Missionary Ridge,* where General George Thomas broke the Confederate siege line; and *Signal Point,* a Union signal post from which the view today includes the "Grand Canyon of the Tennessee" below and to the right, and to the left, Chattanooga and Lookout Mountain in the distance. Open daily 8 A.M. to dusk. Free. Write the park at P.O. Box 2126, Fort Oglethorpe, GA 30741. 404-866-9241.

Cravens House (ca. 1854), off Route 148 on Lookout Mountain, a white clapboard structure built by pioneer industrialist Robert Cravens, was used by both armies as headquarters during the struggle for Chattanooga. Strenuous fighting occurred near the house on October 23, 1863, as Union troops under General Joseph Hooker pushed back the Confederate force on Lookout Mountain. Although damaged in the battle and further despoiled by journalists with the Union army, who stripped materials from it to build summer quarters on the mountain, the house was rebuilt by the Cravens family after the war. Costumed guides show the house and period furnishings. Open March through November Mon.–Sat. 10–5, Sun. 1–5. Nominal charge; children free. 615-821-6161.

Point Park, at the northern crest of Lookout Mountain, offers a panoramic view of the 7-mile bend of the Tennessee River nearly 1,500 feet below. To the right, Chattanooga spreads toward the north and east, and far in the distance the foothills of East Tennessee ascend toward the Appalachian Mountains. At Point Park, monuments, plaques, and the *Ochs Museum* commemorate the "Battle Above the Clouds."

Lookout Mountain Museum, 1110 East Brow Road, across from Point Park, displays life-size dioramas and artifacts from Indian, frontier settlement, and Civil War history. Nominal charge. 615-821-7625.

Rock City Gardens is on Lookout Mountain. There was a time, not long ago, when one could not drive through the American South without encountering roadside and barnside signs urging "See Rock City," and each year more than half a

Point Park, overlooking Chattanooga from Lookout Mountain, is one of eight historic areas constituting the Chickamauga and Chattanooga National Military Park. The great bend of the Tennessee River lies below.

The high bluffs surrounding Chattanooga are a favorite launching place for hang gliders.

million people do. From vantage points in the picturesque rock formations of the mountain, the panorama sweeps over seven states. Visitors follow a flagstone trail, cross a suspension bridge, view a waterfall, and dine in a restaurant built around a rock outcrop. For the delight of children, scenes from nursery rhymes and children's classics are re-created in *Mother Goose Village* and in *Fairyland Caverns* under the mountain. Open daily 8 A.M. to sundown May 21 through Labor Day, 8:30 A.M. to sundown the rest of the year. Fee charged. 404-820-2531.

At the foot of Lookout Mountain, three blocks south of U.S. 11, 41, 64, and 72, is the *Incline Railway Station.* At the top of the mountain, two blocks from historic Point Park, is the railway's *Cloud High Station.* Between them, tracks climb the face of the mountain to an altitude of 2,100 feet. Near the top the grade is 72.7 percent, making this the steepest passenger-incline-railway in the world. When built in 1895, it was powered by steam; now electric, the railway is listed in the National Register of Historic Places. At 8 miles an hour the large passenger cars, with glass astrodome roofs for unobstructed viewing, pass through the site of the "Battle Above the Clouds" and afford spectacular views of the Chattanooga Valley. An observation deck rises above the Cloud High Station, from which hourly in summer an open "surrey" bus leaves on a tour of the mountain and its scenic attractions. Another departs during the summer for Rock City. Ample free parking at the lower station. Frequent trips daily all year. Fee charged. 615-629-1473.

Ruby Falls, on Route 148, is a 145-foot-high natural waterfall, 1,120 feet underground in *Lookout Mountain Caverns.* An elevator carries guided tours to the cave. Fee charged. 615-821-2544. Nearby *Crystal Caverns,* on Cumming Highway 41, include some of the oldest cave formations in Tennessee. Open all year. 615-821-9403.

An early photograph of the Lookout Mountain Incline Railway Number 2 at Chattanooga, taken in 1897, just two years after its construction. The car is approaching the steepest part of the mountain, where the grade is 72.7 percent.

The *Hall of American Presidents Wax Museum,* 3919 Saint Elmo Avenue, at the foot of Lookout Mountain, houses life-size figures of all American presidents and several other famous persons. Open daily May through October, weekends only during the rest of the spring and fall. Nominal charge. 615-821-4907.

The *Confederama,* 3742 Tennessee Avenue, near the Incline Railway at the foot of Lookout Mountain, is a 480-foot-square miniature landscape on which the Civil War battles at Chickamauga and Chattanooga are re-created by 5,000 tiny model soldiers. Open Mon.–Sat. 9–9, Sun. 1–9 in summer; Mon.–Sat. 9–5, Sun. 1–6 in winter. Nominal charge. 615-821-2812.

Reflection Riding, off U.S. 41 and U.S. 11, is a beautifully landscaped 300-acre park on Lookout Creek at the foot of Lookout Mountain. Along winding nature trails, 45 species of trees and 65 varieties of wildflowers have been identified. Open Mon.–Sat. 9 A.M. to dusk, Sun. 1 P.M. to dusk. Nominal charge.

National Cemetery, in downtown Chattanooga, off Bailey Avenue, just east of Central Avenue, was founded in 1863 by order of General George Thomas, then commander of the Union Army of the Cumberland. It is one of the largest and most beautiful cemeteries in the South. Buried here are James J. Andrews and seven of his men. In April 1862, near Marietta, Georgia, Andrews and some twenty Union troops disguised as civilians seized the Confederate steam locomotive "The General" and several boxcars to run toward Chattanooga on a mission to destroy the railroad. At the end of the "Great Locomotive Chase," they were forced to abandon the train near the Tennessee line and these eight were captured and executed in Atlanta as spies. A replica of "The General" stands near their graves. Open daily 8–5. Free.

The *Confederate Cemetery,* founded by returning veterans

in 1865, is between East Third and East Fifth streets, just north of the University of Tennessee at Chattanooga. Open daily 8–5. Free.

At the *Hunter Museum of Art,* 10 Bluff View, American works include nineteenth- and twentieth-century paintings by such artists as Thomas Hart Benton, Winslow Homer, Thomas Sully, and Andrew Wyeth, as well as prints, drawings, and sculpture. The museum is in a *ca.*-1904 Classic Revival mansion built by Coca-Cola magnate George Thomas Hunter on a 90-foot bluff overlooking the Tennessee River. Formerly on the site were a sacred ground of the Cherokee, a Civil War battery location, and an early steel foundry. A contemporary building, built into the bluff below the home, includes five additional galleries. Open Tues.–Sat. 10–4:30, Sun. 1–4:30. Free. 615-267-0968.

The *Harris Swift Museum of Religious Art,* 526 Vine Street, contains artifacts from many religious traditions— Jewish scrolls, life-size Chinese man-gods, figures of Buddha—and a library of rare religious books and manuscripts. Open Mon.–Fri. 9–5. Free.

The *Houston Antique Museum,* 201 High Street, near the University of Tennessee at Chattanooga, displays the personal collections of Anna Safley Houston, who began collecting antiques near the turn of the century and bequeathed her acquisitions to the city on her death in 1951. Her passion was pitchers, and the collection includes some 15,000 of every conceivable kind and material, as well as art glass, Toby jugs, Chinese Export and Blue Staffordshire porcelain, Lustreware, Rogers groups, quilts, early lamps, toys, pewter, Sandwich-glass artist's models, and other objects. It was said of Mrs. Houston that she had "one of everything." The museum is in a *ca.*-1890 brick Victorian home furnished with eighteenth- and nineteenth-century American furniture. Open Tues.–Sat. 10–4:30, Sun. 2–4:30. Closed major holidays. Group

The Tennessee Valley Railroad Museum at Chattanooga is a state museum dedicated to the "golden age of railroading." Visitors may ride the museum's main line and inspect a typical turn-of-the-century depot.

tours Monday by appointment. Nominal charge. 615-267-7176.

"For all the family" accurately describes *The Tennessee Valley Railroad Museum,* the official state railroad museum of Tennessee, just off North Chamberlain Avenue, on the side of Missionary Ridge, ten minutes from downtown Chattanooga. The trains here are the real thing. The collection includes, from the "Golden Age of Steam," locomotives, day coaches, pullman cars, streetcars, a dining car, freight equipment, a caboose, and even rare private cars, all open for inspection. Visitors may board a standard-gauge steam-powered passenger train for a 45-minute, 6-mile round trip through the historic tunnel that played a key role in the Battle of Missionary Ridge, across high bridges and through beautiful scenery to the site of future museum facilities east of the ridge. At the entrance to the Emma Street Yards in east Chattanooga is a replica of a typical 1920s small-town depot. Special events are planned throughout the season. Open May through October Sat. 10–5, Sun. afternoon. Nominal charge for train ride and museum admission. Group tours by reservation. 615-622-5908.

The *Chattanooga Choo-Choo Complex,* 1400 Market Street, is an encouraging example of adaptation and continued use of a grand old building. This Neo-classical Revival terminal, built 1906–08, now houses a 1,350-seat restaurant under the original magnificent 85-foot-high free-standing dome, said to have been the world's highest when the terminal first opened. The terminal warehouse, storage, and baggage buildings now contain shops and lounges, and for overnight accommodations, 24 refurbished railroad sleeper cars have been converted to 48 combination living-bedrooms, furnished in Victorian style complete with brass beds, overstuffed furniture, and turn-of-the-century lamps. A modern motel-hotel building is also in the complex. For a nominal charge visitors may tour the 24-acre complex and the old-fashioned formal gardens aboard one of two restored trolley cars. The *Model Railroad Museum* in the complex consists of a working-scale model of Chattanooga and Lookout Mountain in the era when this was a major rail center. The 175-foot-long layout incorporates more than 3,000 feet of track. Nominal charge. 615-266-6484.

Booker T. Washington Day Use State Park, Route 58, includes 33 campsites and recreational facilities on Chickamauga Lake. Write the park at P.O. Route 2, Box 369, Chattanooga, TN 37416. 615-894-4955.

The *Cumberland State Scenic Trail, Chattanooga Section,* begins in Prentice Cooper State Forest, off Route 27, and continues northward along the Cumberland Plateau to its terminus at the rim of the Sequatchie Valley. Two primitive campsites are located along the trail, a portion of which extends to Signal Point. 615-741-1061.

Further opportunities for amusement in the Chattanooga area incude *Raccoon Mountain Caverns and Skyride,* on U.S. 41, a favorite spot for hang-gliding. Fee charged. 615-821-9403. The 2,350-foot *Alpine Slide* on Raccoon Mountain, U.S. 41, provides a good view of Lookout Mountain across the valley. Fee charged. 615-825-5666. *Lake Winnepesaukah Amusement Park* is nearby on Lakeview Drive, Rossville, Georgia. Nominal charge; organized groups free, 404-866-5681.

For more information about Chattanooga and its vicinity, including southeastern Tennessee and northwestern Georgia, write the Chattanooga Area Convention and Visitors Bureau, 1001 Market Street, Chattanooga, TN 37402. 615-756-2121.

CHEROKEE NATIONAL FOREST The Forest consists of two relatively long and narrow sections of mountainous land along the North Carolina–Tennessee border. From the Great Smoky Mountains National Park, one part of the Forest stretches southwest to the Georgia line and the other lies to the northeast between the park and the Virginia border. The two parcels total 604,000 acres, with many developed and primitive campsites, several substantial lakes, wilderness and scenic areas, and more than 1,000 miles of streams and rivers. Unlike the National Parks, the Forest permits hunting, and game includes black bear, whitetailed deer, ruffed grouse, wild turkey, gray squirrel, red fox, gray fox, raccoon, and European wild boar in the south. Programs are offered at many of the developed recreational areas, including movies, illustrated talks, and forest walks conducted by Forest Service personnel. Camping at developed sites is on a first-come basis; stays are limited to fourteen consecutive days; certain campgrounds charge fees. Write the Forest Supervisor, P.O. Box 400, Cleveland, TN 37311. 615-476-5528.

A 23-mile stretch of the Hiwassee River from the North Carolina line to U.S. 411 in the southern part of the Forest has been declared a State Scenic River and preserved for canoeing, fishing, and primitive camping. The Hiwassee is a very popular place for canoes, rafts, and tubes. For information on access and the many boat rentals write the Ranger Naturalist, P.O. Box 255, Delano, TN 37325. 615-263-1341. The Ocoee River in the Forest is one of the prime white-water rivers in the eastern United States. The North American White Water Championships have been held on the Ocoee, and there are a number of guided-raft-trip operators. A brochure listing river outfitters on all Tennessee rivers is available from the Department of Tourist Development.

CLEVELAND   A *walking tour* of downtown Cleveland, compiled by the Bradley County Historical Society, includes forty landmarks that have played a significant part in the his-

The Copper Basin, a 56-square-mile area southeast of Cleveland near Duck-town, was ravaged by mining practices in the 1870s. The barren hills of the Copper Basin resemble a Western desert set among the green mountains of East Tennessee.

tory of the city. Write the Cleveland Chamber of Commerce, 2100 Keith Street, P.O. Box 1018, Cleveland, TN 37311. 615-472-6587. A *Primitive Settlement,* off U.S. 64E, contains nineteenth-century log cabins gathered from their original locations in the area and restored and refurbished with antique household items, tools, and furniture. The oldest is 150 years old, and each represents a different style of frontier life. Open daily 10–6. Nominal charge. 615-476-5096. The *Copper Basin,* on U.S. 64E in the extreme southeastern corner of Tennessee, is a 56-square-mile area devastated by the copper-mining practices of the 1870s. In 1851, miners began stripping ore from these hills to feed huge open copper roasters. Timber was stripped to fuel the roasters, and the sulfur dioxide fumes the roasters released further strangled the vegetation. Erosion performed the final clearing, eating away the topsoil to leave the barren hills that today resemble a desert. The reds, pinks, and whites of the bare land change hue and color with the seasons and the time of day, much as in the Badlands of South Dakota and the Grand Canyon of Arizona. The mines and roasters have been long abandoned, but their memory is preserved in artifacts and photographs at the *Ducktown Museum.* The community of Ducktown, named for Cherokee Chief Duck, began as the brawling boomtown that grew up near the first of the Copper Basin mines.

CROSSVILLE During the Depression, the Roosevelt administration effected a plan to provide employment and sorely needed housing in this sparsely settled region of Tennessee: 29,000 acres of mostly cut-over land were purchased and divided into small farms of between 5 and 50 acres each. Selected to homestead these farms were 250 families, chosen for their good character, rural background, and desire for self-sufficiency. Barns were constructed first, and the settlers lived in them while they built homes of timber and rock gleaned from the land as it was cleared. Traditional techniques were used in constructing houses: hand-split shingles, hand-hewn oak beams, and hand-wrought ironware. Many of the original homesteaders have moved, but their traditional way of life is reflected in the extraordinary variety of merchandise carried by the *Cumberland General Store,* about 4 miles south of Crossville on U.S. 127 in Homestead: McGuffey Readers, mule bits, horse collars, drawknives, cuspidor brushes, hand-tied tobacco, and thousands more of old-fashioned tools, toys, and appurtenances of rural life. The store will even build on order more than ten separate models of horse-drawn conveyances, from a phaeton to a farm wagon to a surrey with fringe on top. For a fee they will send their 256-page illustrated "Wish & Want Book." Open Mon.–Sat. 7:30–5, Sun. 1–5. Closed major holidays. Write the store at Route 3, Crossville, TN 38555. 615-484-8481.

The *Cumberland Mountain State Rustic Park,* 4 miles south of Crossville on U.S. 127, was created in 1938 as a 1,720-acre recreational area for the homesteaders of Cumberland County. Buildings, constructed by the Civilian Conservation Corps (CCC) and the Work Projects Administration (WPA), are of a local sandstone rock called Crab Orchard Stone. Attractions include 146 campsites, 37 family cabins, a restaurant, 50-acre Cumberland Lake, hiking trails, programs conducted by a seasonal naturalist, and the botanical diversity of the Cumberland Plateau. Open all year. Write the Superintendent's Office, Crossville, TN 38555. 615-484-6138.

The *Cumberland Mountain Craft Association,* on Route 9 in Crossville, is a nonprofit cooperative devoted to promoting traditional crafts by providing a market where native families can demonstrate their skills and sell their creations.

The *Cumberland County Playhouse,* in Crossville, offers professional theater with five major productions each season, ranging from drama to musical comedy.

DAYTON For eight sweltering days in July 1925, the world's attention was focused on the *Rhea County Courthouse* (1890–91), Market Street at Second and Third avenues, the site of the "Monkey Trial," *State of Tennessee* v. *John Thomas Scopes.* In the spring of 1925, the Tennessee legislature had made it illegal for public-school teachers "to teach any theory that denies the story of the Divine Creation of man as taught in the Bible." Several civic leaders in Dayton, motivated in part by a sincere desire to probe the resolve of the law and in part by dreams of the commerce that would accompany such a celebrated trial, persuaded Scopes, a young teacher at the local high school, to lend his name to a test case. The trial proceeded in a circus atmosphere as the curious, and more than a few fanatics, descended on the town. The city fathers appointed a "committee on entertainment for the Scopes trial." WGN Chicago set up the first nationwide radio hookup, and even H. L. Mencken came to Dayton. In the courtroom, two brilliant lawyers—fundamentalist William Jennings Bryan for the prosecution and religious skeptic Clarence Darrow for the defense—met in the dramatic courtroom confrontation upon which the play *Inherit the Wind* was based. Scopes was convicted and the Tennessee Supreme Court later upheld the anti-evolution law while reversing his conviction on a technicality. Bryan died in Dayton five days after the trial. The law, though largely disregarded, remained in force until 1967.

ELIZABETHTON *The Elizabethton Historic District,* roughly bounded by Second, Fourth, East, and Sycamore streets, includes many remaining nineteenth-century structures. Under a sycamore tree is a marker designating the spot where the first court west of the Allegheny Mountains was held, in 1772. The *Doe River covered bridge* on Riverside Drive is exceptionally well preserved. Built in 1882, the 134-foot span was the only county bridge across the Doe to survive the 1901 flood. Closed one year for repairs in 1975, it remains

The Doe River covered bridge, on Riverside Drive at Elizabethton, is believed to be the oldest covered bridge still in use in Tennessee. Built in 1882, the 134-foot span is listed in the Historic American Engineering Record.

Sinking Creek Baptist Church, on U.S. 321 between Elizabethton and Johnson City, is considered to be the oldest standing church in Tennessee.

sound and continues to carry traffic. The *John and Landon Carter Mansion* (1780) is on East Broad Street. John Carter crossed the mountains from Virginia before the Revolution, prospered as a trader, and was a leader of the Watauga Association (see *Sycamore Shoals* below). His son, Landon, was secretary of state of the short-lived State of Franklin and was later implicated in a land fraud with Governor John Sevier, though the accusation was unproved and, at least in part, political. The 2½ story frame and clapboard house, with Georgian elements and elaborate interior woodwork, is one of the oldest houses in Tennessee. Private. *Sinking Creek Baptist Church,* on U.S. 321 between Elizabethton and Johnson City, is a hand-hewn log church considered the oldest standing church in Tennessee.

Sycamore Shoals Historic Site, U.S. 321 on the Watauga River, was the site of Fort Watauga, built in the early 1770s by settlers from Virginia and North Carolina. Because neither state was interested in annexing the Watauga Lands, the settlers met in 1772 at what is now Elizabethton to form the Watauga Association. Their compact for self-government, which provided for the election of five members "to govern and direct for the common good of all people," was one of the first constitutions written independently by Americans. In 1775, the Transylvania Company acquired 20 million acres of the Cumberland River watershed from the Cherokee Indians and resold the land to the Watauga settlers. In the fall of 1780, Britain's Major Patrick Ferguson, leading an army of Loyalists through South and North Carolina in support of Major General Lord Cornwallis, commanded the patriots beyond the mountains to lay down their arms or he would "march his own men over the mountains, hang their leaders, and lay their country waste with fire and sword." Isaac Shelby and John Sevier rallied about a thousand frontiersmen at Sycamore Shoals and on October 7, 1780, after a march of some

Fort Watauga, part of Sycamore Shoals State Historic Site at Elizabethton, was built in the early 1770s by settlers from Virginia and North Carolina. Here settlers met in 1772 to adopt the constitution of the Watauga Association and the "Overmountain Men" gathered in 1780 for the march to Kings Mountain in South Carolina.

ten days over the mountains, attacked Ferguson where he had encamped atop Kings Mountain, a narrow ridge in northwestern South Carolina. After just an hour of hard fighting, Ferguson lay dead and the Loyalists surrendered. This victory by the Overmountain Men was the turning point of the Revolutionary War in the South. A replica of Fort Watauga stands near the fort's original location; historical films are shown at a visitors' center. Open daily 8–5. Free. Write to P.O. Box 1198, Elizabethton, TN 37643. 615-543-5808.

GATLINBURG This town, at the head of the cove through which the Pigeon River runs, is the western entrance and headquarters of the *Great Smoky Mountains National Park* (see GREAT SMOKY MOUNTAINS NATIONAL PARK). The streets of Gatlinburg are shoulder to shoulder with commercial tourist attractions catering to the more than 8 million people who visit the park annually. For information on events, attractions, and accommodations in the Gatlinburg vicinity, visit the Chamber of Commerce at 520 Parkway, or write them at Gatlinburg, TN 37738. 615-436-4178. Outside Tennessee call toll-free 1-800-251-9868.

Christus Gardens, River Road, in a long, low structure of Tennessee and Georgia marble, depicts through life-size figures in authentic settings important events in the life of Christ. Choral music, dramatic lighting, and informative narrative blend to bring to life such scenes as the Nativity, the Sermon on the Mount, and the Last Supper. The figures are crafted by accomplished artists and clothed in faithful reproductions of biblical-period clothing, fashioned from fabric woven in the area of the Holy Land country that each figure represents. The rotunda displays the nation's most complete collection of coins of biblical times and countries. During the winter, the collection goes on tour. Open daily 8–10 early spring to late fall; open as posted late fall to early spring. Special rates for children. 615-436-5155.

Ober-Gatlinburg Ski Resort, a ski area with four slopes serviced by chair lifts and rope tows, has night skiing and snow-making capability. The expert slope is 4,800 feet with a vertical drop of 800 feet. There is a year-round Alpine sledride, a bobsled-type ride that careens down a half-mile run. One slope has an artificial surface for year-round skiing, and a ski school and rentals are available. Write the resort at Gatlinburg, TN 37738. 615-436-5423.

Adventures of America, in downtown Gatlinburg, brings vicarious thrills to even the timid. A giant spherical movie screen creates the illusion of a succession of dangerous adventures: Take a helicopter through the Grand Canyon, fly over Niagara Falls, or ride a runaway trolley. Shows are given every twenty minutes. Nominal charge. Group rates. 615-436-4663.

A new attraction, *Gatlinburg Place,* is a $10 million family-entertainment complex featuring an IMAX theater with the world's largest movie screen, 7 stories high and nearly 100 feet wide. It shows a 70mm movie, *To Fly,* produced for the National Air and Space Museum in Washington, D.C. There are live musical shows in the evenings and an animated "Backwoods Bear Jamboree," similar to ones at Disney World and Disneyland. Open daily. Admission charge.

The *American Historical Wax Museum,* on the Parkway, has 45 separate scenes peopled by more than 130 individual life-sized costumed figures including a section devoted to Tennessee history. Open daily 9–5, evenings until 11, May through October. Fee charged. Group rates available. 615-436-4462.

The *World of Illusions,* 716 Parkway, depicts the practice of magic from 3,000 B.C. through a series of action illusions. Admission charge. 615-436-9701.

The *World of the Unexplained Museum,* Parkway at River Road, presents exhibits of extrasensory perception, magic,

The town of Gatlinburg is a gateway to the Great Smoky Mountains.

Several aerial lifts in the Gatlinburg area afford panoramic views of the town and the nearby Great Smoky Mountains.

Hundreds of miles of foot and horse trails penetrate the Great Smoky Mountains National Park on the Tennessee–North Carolina border. More than a thousand species of flowering plants grow on these mountains, and other flora are found in similar abundance and variety.

and the occult. Open all year. Fee charged. 615-436-5019.

Ripley's Believe It or Not Museum, on the Parkway, features twelve galleries with more than five hundred examples of the odd and unusual from the collection of Robert Ripley. Open all year. Fee charged; group rates available. 615-436-5096.

The *Guinness Hall of World Records,* on the Parkway, offers exhibits from the Guinness Book of Records. Fee charged. 615-436-9100.

The *Sweet Fanny Adams Theatre,* 461 Parkway, presents musical comedy nightly at 8:30 mid-May through October. Fee charged. 615-436-4039.

The *Gatlinburg Space Needle,* on the Parkway, affords a panoramic view of the city and the Great Smoky Mountains to the east. A glass-enclosed elevator ascends to the observation deck. Open all year. Nominal charge. 615-436-4629.

The *Gatlinburg Sky Lift* carries passengers up Crockett Mountain to a promontory overlooking the city. Operates early spring through late summer. Fee charged. 615-436-4307.

Other family amusements in Gatlinburg include: the *Gatlinburg Aerial Tramway* to the ski resort (Fee charged. 615-436-4440); the *Eagle Top Lift* (Nominal charge. 615-436-4117); and the *Gatlinburg Water Slide* (Fee charged. 615-436-6362).

Many of the trails in the National Park are open to horse-back riders, and the mountains near Gatlinburg are threaded with scenic riding trails. Several nearby stables rent mounts. McCarter Stables, in the park on U.S. 441 South near park headquarters, is open daily April through October. 615-436-5354. Smoky Mountain Riding Stables, 4 miles east of downtown Gatlinburg on Route 73, also rents horses for both beginning and experienced riders. 615-436-5634.

GREAT SMOKY MOUNTAINS NATIONAL PARK Astride the Tennessee–North Carolina border, this

The Great Smoky Mountains, rugged yet verdant, cover more than half a million acres of land. The mysterious blue-gray haze often seen blanketing their valleys and summits gives these mountains, called by the native Cherokee "Land of the Great Smoke," their name.

is the most heavily visited of all the national parks, and yet its vast size and rugged terrain still offer solitude and adventure to the backwoods camper. Within its 643 square miles, elevations range from 857 feet along the Little Tennessee River upward to 6,642 feet at the summit of Clingmans Dome, with sixteen peaks above 6,000 feet. The variety of altitudes, temperate climate, and abundant rainfall produce an astonishing diversity of flora. Among the park's more than 3,500 species of plant life are 130 species of trees, more than 1,400 species of flowering plants, and more than 300 species of mosses and liverworts. Two hundred thousand acres of virgin hardwoods constitute perhaps our finest remaining Temperate Zone deciduous forest. The mountains are enjoyable all year: Seasonal attractions include blooming wildflowers and migrating birds in April and May; cool temperatures and blooming mountain laurel and rhododendron in May, June, and July; and the glorious colors of the hardwood forests on clear October days.

More than 800 miles of foot and horse trails traverse the park, and camping is permitted in seven developed campgrounds, with all the usual facilities, in primitive campsites along the backcountry trails and even away from the trails. There is a daily charge at sites in developed campgrounds. Three popular campgrounds—Cades Cove, Elkmont, and Smokemont—operate on a computerized advance-reservation system from May through October. Reservations for these are not accepted by phone; they may be made in person at the park or at any Ticketron outlet nationwide, and they may be obtained by mail (allow six weeks) from Ticketron Reservation System, P.O. Box 19992, Washington, D.C. 20036. All other campgrounds operate on a first-come basis. A backcountry camping permit, available free from any visitors' center or ranger station, is required for all overnight hiking parties. Those hardy souls who want to travel off the

The high mountains of the Great Smoky Mountains National Park isolate the fertile valley of Cades Cove.

The home of John Oliver, the first known settler in Cades Cove. Today Cades Cove is part of the Great Smoky Mountains National Park and is leased for farming under strict regulations that preserve its nineteenth-century atmosphere.

marked trails will be granted a camping permit allowing them to camp anywhere in the park, as long as their camp is sufficiently removed from any trail or developed area. From November through March, backcountry permits will be granted only after the park ranger is convinced that your equipment, provisions, and experience are equal to the severe weather. A free leaflet, "Backcountry Map and Camping Guide," is available at any ranger station or visitors' center.

The many miles of cold, clear freestone streams in the park offer some of the finest opportunities in the Southeast to fish for rainbow and brown trout in a wilderness setting. A state license, but no special permit, is required.

The entrances to the park from Tennessee are at Gatlinburg, where the Newfound Gap Road, the only paved road crossing the park, begins its climb across the gap to Cherokee, North Carolina, and at Townsend. Park headquarters and the Sugarlands Visitor Center are 2 miles south of Gatlinburg on the Newfound Gap Road.

At *Mount Le Conte* (6,593 feet), the Le Conte Lodge offers accommodations within the park mid-April to late October; its serenity is preserved by the half-day hike necessary to reach it. For reservations, write Le Conte Lodge, Gatlinburg, TN 37738. A paved road reaches Elkmont, where hotel accommodations are available June 1 to October 31.

In *Cades Cove,* in the western end of the park, where the Park Service has re-created farmsteads much like those spread throughout the valleys and coves of these mountains before the park was created in 1940, an 11-mile loop road passes log cabins and split-rail fences. Bicycles, a popular way to explore the cove, can be rented at the visitors' center.

Many of the park's trails are open to saddle horses, which are available for hire during the temperate months at Cades Cove, Dudley Creek, Cosby, Two Mile Branch, and in North Carolina at Smokemont. For information or camping reservations, write the Superintendent, Great Smoky Mountains National Park, Gatlinburg, TN 37738. 615-436-5615. The U.S. Geological Survey publishes a handsome shaded relief map of the park and vicinity ("Great Smoky Mountains National Park and Vicinity, North Carolina–Tennessee," relief edition, scale 1:125,000) and another, on a much more intimate scale, in two sheets ("Great Smoky Mountains National Park [east and west halves] North Carolina–Tennessee," scale 1:62,500). These are available from the U.S. Geological Survey Distribution Section, 1200 South Eads Street, Arlington, VA 22202. 703-557-2751.

GREENEVILLE Named for the Revolutionary War general Nathanael Greene, Greeneville was founded sometime after 1783 by Scotch-Irish settlers and in 1785 became the last capital of the short-lived State of Franklin. A log-cabin replica and a marker, off Route 70 northwest of town, commemorate Greeneville's service as capital of this experiment in frontier independence. The town prospered commercially from its location on early stage- and trade-routes and was admitted to the Union as part of Tennessee in 1796.

The *Greeneville Historic District,* a business district surrounded by residential areas, includes numerous eighteenth- to twentieth-century commercial, residential, and religious structures. The Federal *Sevier House* was the home of Valentine Sevier, whose brother, John Sevier, was the instigator of Franklin and later the first governor of Tennessee. The Greek Revival *First Presbyterian Church* (1912) is a copy of its 1780 predecessor.

The *Andrew Johnson National Historic Site* is really three separate areas scattered throughout the city of Greeneville. Johnson, a native of Raleigh, North Carolina, moved to Greeneville in 1826 at the age of seventeen. He left school, supported his family as a tailor, educated himself, entered politics, was elected alderman, mayor, governor, congress-

Andrew Johnson, who would become the seventeenth president of the United States, came to Greeneville in 1826 at the age of seventeen and worked as a tailor before embarking on his political career. His home, restored to the 1869–75 period, is one of three places making up the Andrew Johnson National Historic Site.

man, senator, and vice-president, and became the seventeenth president of the United States after the assassination of Abraham Lincoln on April 14, 1865. The visitor center complex, at the corner of Depot and College streets, includes a museum and the *tailor shop* in which Johnson worked from 1831 to 1843. The house in which he lived from the 1830s until 1851 has yet to be restored. The *Andrew Johnson Homestead,* on Main Street, was the family home from 1851 to 1875 and has been restored to appear as it did when Johnson returned from Washington in 1869. He is buried in the *Andrew Johnson National Cemetery,* one block east of West Main Street. The grave is marked by a slender marble column, crowned with an American eagle and engraved with a scroll symbolizing the United States Constitution. All three areas of the Historic Site are open daily 9–5. A nominal admission fee is charged to adults at the homestead from June 1 through September 15. Other times and other areas are free. 615-638-3503.

Davy Crockett Birthplace Park is east of Greeneville off U.S. 11E and U.S. 411 at Limestone. David Crockett (1786–1836), frontiersman, wit, hero of the Creek Indian War (1813–14), state legislator, three-term U.S. congressman, rival to Andrew Jackson, and martyr in the cause of Texas independence at the Alamo, was born on the banks of the Nolichucky River, near the present town of Limestone, Tennessee. A replica of the log cabin in which he was born, a picnic area, and a shelter are surrounded by a rail fence. Open daily 8 A.M.–10 P.M. mid-May to October 1; daily 8–5 October 1 through May 14. Free.

HARRISON *Harrison Bay State Day Use Park,* northeast of Chattanooga off Route 58, includes 39 miles of shore on Chickamauga Lake and has the most complete docking facilities available on any TVA lake, including a marina with a restaurant. There are 260 wooded campsites. Open March through October. Write the park at Harrison, TN 37341. 615-344-6214.

HARROGATE   The *Abraham Lincoln Museum* is on the campus of Lincoln Memorial University, founded in 1898 and dedicated to Lincoln in appreciation of his concern for the people of East Tennessee and eastern Kentucky. The museum has more than a quarter of a million items in one of the country's largest collections of artifacts belonging to Lincoln or relating to his period. Open in summer Mon.–Sat. 10–6, Sun. 1–6; September through May Tues.–Sat. 9–4. Nominal charge. Group rates and other hours by appointment. 615-869-3614.

Cumberland Gap National Historic Park is half a mile northwest of Cumberland Gap on U.S. 25E. In his landmark essay on the significance of the frontier in American history, Frederick Jackson Turner wrote, "Stand at Cumberland Gap and watch the procession of civilization, marching single file—the buffalo following the trail to the salt springs, the Indian, the fur-trader and hunter, the cattle-raiser, the pioneer farmer—and the frontier has passed by." Discovered in 1674 by an illiterate frontiersman, Gabriel Arthur, this gap was the first great breach to be found in the forbidding Allegheny Mountains, which had barred the west from settlement. Rediscovered and named in 1750 by Dr. Thomas Walker, this natural passage through the mountains at the conjunction of Tennessee, Kentucky, and Virginia became the funnel through which the westward movement passed. In 1775 Daniel Boone, as an employee of the Transylvania Company, led a party of axmen that hewed a part of the wilderness road through the gap. After the Revolutionary War, thousands of settlers followed his trail into the bluegrass region of Kentucky, and Cumberland Gap remained the principal passage over the mountains until more direct routes were opened in the nineteenth century. During the Civil war,

Cumberland Gap was a strategic military position coveted by both North and South. The National Historic Park includes parts of Tennessee, Kentucky, and Virginia, a total of 32 square miles, including 2 miles of the Wilderness Road, the ruins of an early iron furnace, and Civil War fortifications. The three states, which can be seen from the Pinnacle, meet at *Tri-State Peak*. Open daily 8:30–5 November through May; daily 8–6 June through October. Free. Write the park at P.O. Box 840, Middlesboro, KY 40965. 606-248-2817.

JEFFERSON CITY *Glenmore* (1868–69), off U.S. 11E at the eastern edge of Jefferson City, is among the finest Second Empire residences in Tennessee. With its mansard roof, arched windows, wraparound porch, three-story entrance tower, and irregular shape, it is a magnificent example of the pleasing eccentricities of Victorian architecture. Because the twenty-seven-room brick mansion was impossible to heat, the family spent the winter in a smaller replica of Glenmore, which adjoined it in the rear. Open Sat. and Sun. 1–5. Admission charge. An APTA property.

JELLICO *Indian Mountain State Camping Park,* off I-75 between Jellico and the Kentucky border, is a small 213-acre park built on a reclaimed strip-mining site. It offers 50 developed campsites, a short nature trail, and rowboat rentals. Write Cove Lake State Day Use Park, Caryville, TN 37714. 615-424-7958.

JOHNSON CITY The *Tipton-Haynes Farm,* just off U.S. 23/19W near the southern edge of Johnson City, was acquired by Colonel John Tipton, a native of Baltimore, in 1784. At the Battle of the State of Franklin, fought here in 1788, Tipton, as Washington County colonel of militia, opposed the faction supporting the independent State of Franklin. In the 1830s, David Haynes purchased the farm as a wedding present for his son, Landon Carter Haynes, an attorney and gifted orator who served as a senator to the Confederacy

The historic Tipton-Haynes Farm at Johnson City represents two prominent East Tennessee families and four distinct periods of Tennessee history.

and lost his property when the South rejoined the Union. The house is restored to the Haynes period and incorporates the old Tipton house; the farm and outbuildings have been re-created as a nineteenth-century working farm. Haynes's law office, called a perfect example of Greek Revival architecture, has also been restored. Open Mon.–Fri. 10–6, Sat. and Sun. 2–6. Nominal charge. 615-926-3631.

Carroll Reece Museum, on the campus of East Tennessee State University, includes exhibits of paintings, graphics, history, music, and textiles, and Tennessee crafts, costumes, and folklore. Open Mon.–Fri. 8–4:45, Sat. and Sun. 1–5. Free.

Rocky Mount (1770–72) on U.S. 11E between Johnson City and Bristol in the vicinity of Piney Flats, was built by William Cobb, one of the earliest Tennessee settlers, justice of the peace in Washington County, and one of the first commissioners of Jonesboro. The house, a nine-room, two-story structure of white oak logs named for the large limestone rocks in the area, served as the capitol of the first recognized government west of the Allegheny Mountains. In 1790, when William Blount was appointed territorial governor of the Territory of the United States South of the River Ohio, he made his home with the Cobb family, conducting territorial affairs from Rocky Mount until a capitol was arranged in Knoxville. The house, which had glass windows, rare on the frontier in this period, has been restored to its eighteenth-century appearance and contains three pieces of original furniture. The separate kitchen, smokehouse, and slave quarters have been restored.

The *Massengill Museum of Overmountain History* contains items from the East Tennessee frontier and serves as a visitor center for Rocky Mount. Open daily April–October; open weekdays January 15 through March and November 1 through 15. Closed November 15 through January 15. Hours: Mon.–Sat. 10–5, Sun. 2–6. Nominal charge. Groups half price. 615-538-7396.

JONESBORO   The oldest town in Tennessee and the scene of some of the most memorable events in the early history of the region, Jonesboro has retained its historic atmosphere. Chartered as "Jonesborough" by the North Carolina legislature in 1779, it became the seat of Washington County, which included all the settlements in what is now Tennessee. The first public building, a log courthouse, was built in 1779, and by 1800, the year Nashborough (Nashville) was founded, more than a hundred homes stood along Jonesboro's single street. At Jonesboro, in 1784, the independent State of Franklin was created. Here Andrew Jackson was admitted to the bar in 1788 and practiced for several years. Two of the first periodicals in the nation to advocate the abolition of slavery were published in Jonesboro, by Elihu Embree: the *Manumission Intelligencer* in 1819 and the *Emancipator* in 1820.

The *Jonesboro Historic District* concentrates its historic buildings along a five-block stretch of Main Street. From its inception, Jonesboro was a planned community. The owner of each lot was allowed to build "one brick, stone, or well-framed house, 20 feet long and 16 feet wide, at least 10 feet in the pitch, with a brick or stone chimney," and any failure to comply brought forfeiture of his land title. Between 1820 and 1855, Jonesboro grew rapidly, and many of the original wooden buildings were replaced with brick structures. Because architectural styles were shifting rapidly in these years, the architecture of Jonesboro is an intriguing mixture of often contrasting styles: modified Georgian, Federal, Greek Revival, Gothic Revival, and even Italianate and Victorian. Two or more styles can be found in a single structure, such as the Italianate porch on the Federal *Robert May House.* The Methodist and Presbyterian churches on West Main Street date from this period. Presidents Andrew Jackson, James K. Polk, and Andrew Johnson are said to have lodged at the *Chester Inn,* built in 1797, with its full-length second-story porch. *Sis-*

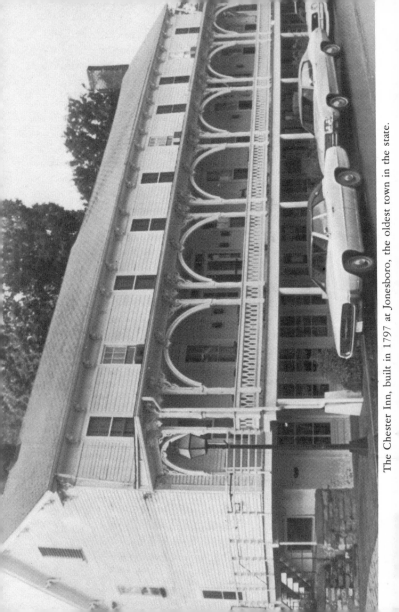

The Chester Inn, built in 1797 at Jonesboro, the oldest town in the state.

Sisters' Row, a brick row house built during the 1820s, is the oldest brick structure in Jonesboro. A Philadelphian built it to provide each of his daughters with a separate home.

Every October spellbinders from around the country meet in Jonesboro to swap yarns at the National Storytelling Festival.

ters' Row, built in the 1820s, is the oldest surviving brick building. A brochure outlining a walking tour is available at the information center and at various local businesses. Twice each year, during Jonesborough Days—a four-day festival ending on the Fourth of July—and at Christmas, a number of historic private homes are open to the public. In October, the *National Storytelling Festival* brings storytellers to Jonesboro to swap yarns. Write the Jonesboro Visitors Bureau, Box 375, Jonesboro, TN 37659.

KINGSPORT   On the Holston River, surrounded by the southern Appalachians, Kingsport began as a frontier settlement on Long Island (see below) in 1761, grew gradually after Cherokee resistance was squelched in 1776, and remained a small trading village until this century. In 1915, city planner John Nolen was engaged to plan an industrial community of 50,000 at Kingsport. In his plan, streets were to radiate from a central town circle, with ample provision for parks and recreation areas interspersed with commercial and residential sections. In the industrial growth that ensued, the plan was often forgotten, but one vestige remains—the *Church Circle District* along Sullivan Street in the center of Kingsport. Four churches surround a circular park at the heart of this 1915–30 business district. Commercial and public buildings in Georgian and Jacobean Revival style, some now converted into offices and stores, convey a sense of the original concept.

Among the historic buildings in Kingsport are the *Clinch-field Railroad Station (ca.* 1905), 101 East Main Street, which spurred industry by providing an outlet to the Great Lakes and Atlantic shipping centers, and the *Old Kingsport Presbyterian Church* (1845–51), Stone Drive, the oldest church in the city.

Allandale, on U.S. 11W 5 miles west of downtown Kingsport, is the elegant former home of the late Harvey C.

Brooks, a prominent Kingsport businessman who bred Tennessee walking horses and Angus cattle on the surrounding farm. The house, which incorporates salvaged elements of an 1847 Knoxville mansion, is furnished with antiques and surrounded by acres of landscaped gardens featuring boxwoods. Open April through October Tues.–Sat. 9:30–4. Open Sun. 1:30–4:30 all year. Nominal charge. Group rates and special tours by appointment. 615-246-8162.

Exchange Place, 4812 Orebank Road, was the nineteenth-century farm of John S. Gaines, who also operated a stage stop and a store where currency was exchanged in the era when Tennessee had its own monetary system. The original log house is incorporated into the present two-story structure, and the springhouse, smokehouse, and barn remain. It is now a craft center with demonstrations and sales of traditional crafts. Open summer Sun. 2–4:30; other times by appointment. 615-288-6613 or 288-5182.

Netherland Inn, 2144 Netherland Inn Road, 2 miles northwest of Kingsport, is an early-nineteenth-century riverfront inn on the Great Stage Road, a principal frontier thoroughfare through Tennessee and Kentucky. Built originally as a dwelling, the stone and frame Federal inn was purchased in 1818 by Richard Netherland. Restored properties include the inn, a stable, a warehouse, slave cabins, a smokehouse, a wharf, a well house, and a flatboat. Open Sun. 2–4:30 May through October, other times by appointment. Nominal charge. 615-246-2662, 247-3211, or 246-6635.

Bays Mountain Park, off Reservoir Road, a city-owned 3,000-acre wilderness park, has a full schedule of interpretative nature programs as well as a nature center, guided nature walks, 25 miles of hiking trails, an amphitheater, nature classes, an exhibit gallery, and live native animals. A planetarium with six-thousand-star capability gives daily shows, and there is a festival of educational activities the first two weekends in May. Open Mon.–Sat. 8:30–8, Sun. 1–8; the nature center opens Sat. 1 P.M. Nominal charges for parking and planetarium.

Warrior's Path State Day Use Park, at Fort Patrick Henry Lake on U.S. 23, has a golf course, swimming, fishing, boating, picnicking, hiking trails, and a campground with 160 sites. Write the park at P.O. Box 5026, Kingsport, TN 37663; phone 615-239-8531.

Long Island of the Holston, on the south fork of the Holston River, was an eighteenth-century gathering place of the Cherokee until the Battle of Long Island Flats on July 20, 1776, which diminished Cherokee participation in the American Revolution. The battle resulted in the Treaty of Long Island by which Cherokee land was ceded to the United States. The island, a small part of which was recently returned to the Cherokee, is largely occupied by private corporations.

KNOXVILLE From May through October 1982, Knoxville hosts the 1982 World's Fair, the first official world's fair since 1975 and the first sanctioned by the Bureau of International Expositions in Paris ever to be held in the southeastern United States. More than 11 million visitors are expected at the 70-acre site along the Tennessee River between downtown Knoxville and the main campus of the University of Tennessee. A 70-foot-high aerial gondola, a chairlift, a tramway, and a riverboat along the Tennessee River will transport visitors around the Fair. Energy, the theme of the Fair, will be symbolized by the Sunsphere, a 266-foot-high tower surmounted by a huge globe encased in 24-karat gold-dust glass. Inside will be a restaurant and three observation decks overlooking the mile-long site. More than twenty nations will participate with exhibits emphasizing their cultures, resources, and future energy strategies. Among the international participants will be Italy, France, the Federal Republic of Germany, a consortium of ten European nations, the United Kingdom, Japan, Australia, Mexico, Saudi Arabia, the Republic of Korea, Canada, the Hungarian People's Republic, and the People's Republic of China (which will be participating in a world's fair for the first time in its history). The United States Pavilion, at one end of a 1,200-foot-long man-made lake, is a six-story cantilevered structure powered by the sun with five exhibit levels. The state of American technology will be represented by numerous corporate exhibitors, and a variety of cultural events and exhibitions will be sponsored by corporate, civic, religious, and municipal groups. There will be international entertainment, shopping areas and restaurants, frequent sporting events, and a daily fireworks display. The Family Funfair, an amusement area along the Tennessee River, will feature fifteen major rides, including the largest operating Ferris wheel in the United States and several new rides never before seen in this country. Twelve historic buildings have been refurbished and adapted to contemporary use, including the Louisville and Nashville Railway Depot, the L&N Hotel, a 1920s confectionery, an antebellum foundry, and seven Victorian homes.

After the fair closes, its site will serve a variety of residual purposes. The city of Knoxville will gain a 6½-acre city park around the central Waters of the World Lake and a convention hall. The University of Tennessee will acquire the amusement area along the waterfront and several of the international pavilions. The area occupied by most of the pavilions will be commercially developed for housing. The Sunsphere will continue as a restaurant and tourist attraction, and the United States Pavilion will remain.

The 1982 World's Fair runs from May 1 through October 31, daily from 10 A.M. to 10 P.M. The one-day admission fee is $9.95 for adults, $9.25 for adults over fifty-five, and $8.25 for children age four to eleven. A two-day ticket is $15.95 for everyone; children age three and under are admitted free.

Season passes are also available, offering significant savings for frequent visitors. Tickets and passes admit the bearer to the fairgrounds and to all exhibits, shows, and events. Amusement rides, food, and souvenirs are priced separately. Tickets are available at the World's Fair, in advance at Ticketron outlets, and by mail from The 1982 World's Fair, Department TC, P.O. Box 1982, Knoxville, TN 37901. The prudent visitor will book accommodations in advance. To make reservations at any area hotel, phone 615-971-1000. Another central reservation number, 615-971-4000, will handle such alternative housing as campgrounds, private homes, apartments, and dormitories. For those wishing to stay outside Knoxville, shuttle service will be available from nearby cities.

Visitors should also contact Knoxvisit, 901 East Summit Hill Drive, which provides maps and brochures of local and regional points of interest, a monthly calendar of special events, and information on accommodations and travel services, including tours offered by several bus lines. Write Knoxvisit at P.O. Box 15012, Knoxville, TN 37901. 615-523-7263.

During the Revolution, Congress and several states with western territories offered grants of land as an inducement to join the Continental Army. North Carolina offered grants as large as twelve thousand acres. James White, a former captain in the Continental Army, explored the Knoxville region in the summer of 1783 in search of land he could claim, and in 1786 he built a settlement on the bank of the Tennessee River. He was soon followed by other claimants, and his settlement was chosen as the capital of the Territory of the United States South of the River Ohio by Governor William Blount, who urged White to lay out streets. The new town was named Knoxville in honor of Secretary of War Henry Knox. In 1795, the old Walton Road, a wagon road from Knoxville to Nashville, was completed; about that same time, the Knoxville Road linked the Wilderness Road to the Cumberland settlements. At the start of the nineteenth century, Knoxville was a rowdy frontier town, the jumping-off place for the interior. In 1796, Tennessee was admitted to the Union, and Knoxville served as the first capital until 1812 and again as capital in 1817–18. The city was under siege during the Civil War and damage was extensive, but unlike many other Southern cities, Knoxville had relied for its sustenance on trade and industry rather than on the plantation system, and postwar recovery was rapid. Knoxville is the home of the University of Tennessee and the Tennessee Valley Authority.

The *Blount Mansion* (1792), 200 West Hill Avenue at the corner of State Street near the courthouse, one of the first frame houses west of the Allegheny Mountains, was the home of Territorial Governor William Blount and served as the territorial capitol. The furnishings are typically Southern in origin, with furniture styles ranging from Jacobean to early Hepplewhite and including a variety of Windsor and Shaker chairs. Also on view are examples of eighteenth-century American glass, English earthenware, and Chinese Export porcelain. Outbuildings include the kitchen, reconstructed on its original foundations, the cooling room, and the office where the affairs of the territory were administered and the constitution of the State of Tennessee was written. The *Craighead-Jackson House* (1818), distinguished by elaborate woodwork, now serves as a visitors' center for the Blount Mansion. Open March through October Tues.–Sat. 9:30–5; May through October Sun. 2–5; November through February Tues.–Sat. 9:30–4:30. Nominal charge. 615-525-2375.

Crescent Bend, the Armstrong-Lockett House (1834), 2728 Kingston Pike, houses an extensive collection of American and English furniture and examples of English silver made between 1670 and 1820. The house, once the center of a working farm of 600 acres, overlooks a bend of the Tennes-

Built in 1792, Knoxville's Blount Mansion was one of the first frame houses constructed west of the Allegheny Mountains. As the home of William Blount, when he was governor of the Territory of the United States South of the River Ohio, it served as the territorial capitol.

see River. Open Tues.–Sat. 10–4, Sun. 1–4. Nominal charge; children free. 615-637-3163.

Confederate Memorial Hall, 3148 Kingston Pike, is a fifteen-room antebellum mansion used by Confederate General James Longstreet as headquarters during his siege of Knoxville in November 1862. Now owned by the United Daughters of the Confederacy, it is furnished appropriately to the Civil War era and houses period artifacts and a library of books and documents pertaining to the South. Open fall and winter Tues.–Sun. 1–4, spring and summer Tues.–Sun. 2–6. Nominal charge. 615-522-2371.

James White Fort, East Hill Avenue, is named for James White, a former soldier in the Continental Army. In 1786, he built a one-and-a-half-story log cabin near here and became the first permanent settler of Knoxville. When he added additional cabins and connected them with a log palisade, his enclave, which served as a repair and restocking point for westbound wagon trains, became known as White's Fort. Here, in 1791, William Blount signed the Treaty of the Holston with the Cherokee, dictating cession of Indian lands. This reconstruction of the fort, close to the original site, includes a museum, a blacksmith shop, and smoke and loom houses. Open Mon.–Sat. 9:30–5, Sun. 1–5. Nominal charge; group rates available. 615-525-6514.

The *John Sevier farm,* on Neubert Springs Road off John Sevier Highway, is the restored home of Colonel John Sevier, the dominant figure of early Tennessee history. Cunning, hot-tempered, and forceful, Sevier was an Indian-fighter, a Revolutionary War hero at Kings Mountain, a land speculator, and the most powerful eighteenth-century political figure on the Appalachian frontier. He was the elected governor of the short-lived independent State of Franklin and the first governor of the State of Tennessee. Open Mon.–Sat. 10–noon, Sun. 2–5. Nominal charge; group rates by appointment. 615-573-5508.

The reconstructed James White Fort stands in downtown Knoxville a few hundred yards from its original site. James White's cabin and palisaded enclosure became a major trading post on the frontier and the beginning of the city of Knoxville.

Marble Springs, the home of Tennessee's first governor, John Sevier, is

Speedwell Manor, off U.S. 129 (Alcoa Highway) in Lakemore Hills, is a historical museum. Open Tues., Thurs., and Sun. 1–5. Nominal charge; children free with an adult; group tours and rates available.

The *Ramsey House* (1797), southeast of Knoxville on Thorngrove Pike, is constructed of fieldstone, with belt courses and jack arches of contrasting stone. It was designed and built by the English architect Thomas Hope for Francis Alexander Ramsey, a county and state official who later served on the board of trustees of Blount College, predecessor of the University of Tennessee. Open Tues.–Sat. 10–5. Nominal charge; children under six free. Groups should make reservations. 615-546-0745.

The *First Presbyterian Church* (1901), 620 State Street, houses the oldest congregation in Knoxville. The first church building was completed in 1816 on a site donated by James White, founder of the city and a presiding elder of the church. A succeeding structure was used by the Union army as a barracks and hospital. The present yellow brick church was completed in 1901. James White and William Blount are buried in the churchyard.

The *Jackson Avenue Warehouse District* is a relatively unaltered area of late-nineteenth- and early-twentieth-century brick warehouses, many with brick, stone, or terra-cotta trim, large brick or metal cornices, and cast-iron ground floors.

Among the finer old public buildings in Knoxville are the marble Renaissance Revival *Old Post Office Building* (1869–73), Clinch and Market Streets, and the *Knoxville City Hall* (1848–51), City Hall Park on Western Avenue, one of the few local examples of Greek Revival architecture, built originally as the Tennessee School for the Deaf.

The *Dulin Gallery of Art,* 3100 Kingston Pike, has a collection of contemporary prints, drawings, and paintings and the Thorne Miniature Rooms housed in the H. L. Dulin

House, the Neo-classical Revival home built in 1915–16 for wealthy businessman Hanson Lee Dulin. The house is an excellent example of the work of architect John Russell Pope. Open Tues.–Fri. noon–4, Sat. and Sun. 1–5. Free. 615-525-6101.

The *Phoenix Gallerie,* 5130 Kingston Pike in Homburg Place, offers original paintings, sculpture, pottery, blown glass, handmade jewelry, and weavings by local artists. Open Mon.–Sat. 9:30–5:30. Free.

The *Beck Cultural Exchange Center,* 1927 Dandridge Avenue, S.E., houses changing art exhibits and permanent collections including perspectives on black history in Tennessee since 1850. Open Tues.–Sat. 10–6. Free. 615-524-8461.

The *Knoxville Arts Council* is a source of information on other arts activities, including performances by the Knoxville Symphony Orchestra and Choral Society. 615-523-2151, ext. 204.

Chilhowee Amusement Park, 3300 Magnolia Avenue, features rides, games, and entertainment. Open Fri. 6 P.M. to midnight, Sat. and Sun. noon to midnight. Admission free, charge for rides. Recreation park open daily all year. 615-637-5840.

The *Knoxville Zoological Park,* adjacent to Chilhowee Park, shelters more than a thousand animals, including one of the largest arrays of exotic big cats in the nation, and offers an unusual reptile complex and a petting zoo for children. Open daily 10–6. Fee charged; children under three, senior citizens, and handicapped free.

The *Students' Museum,* 516 Beamon Street in Chilhowee Park, contains regular exhibits in the physical, life, and earth sciences, mathematics, transportation, communications, Indians, and coins. The *Akima Planetarium* presents changing shows Sat. and Sun. 2:30 P.M. Museum open Mon.–Sat. 9–5, Sun. 2–5. Closed major holidays. Later hours may be arranged for telescope viewing. Nominal charge. 615-637-1121.

Ijams Nature Center, 2914 Island Home Avenue, is a 26-acre park with nature trails described by a brochure for self-guiding tours. Open daily. Free.

The *University of Tennessee* was established in 1794 as Blount College and assumed its present name in 1879. For a tour of the main campus on Cumberland Avenue phone the director of admissions at 615-974-2184.

The *Frank H. McClung Museum,* Circle Park Drive on the University of Tennessee campus, has collections in anthropology, archaeology, fine arts, science, history, and natural history, and the largest collection in the middle South of southeastern Indian archeological material. Open Mon.–Fri. 9–5. Closed major holidays. Free. 615-974-2144.

The *Hopkins Library* of the University of Tennessee includes the books, documents, and political memorabilia of U.S. Senator Estes Kefauver. Open Mon.–Fri. 9–5:30, Sat. 9–noon. Closed Sat. May to October. Free. 615-974-4480.

The *Clarence Brown Theatre, Theatre II,* and the *Carousel Theatre*—all on the University campus—present nine shows annually, produced by two major companies, one professional and another amateur, and by theater students. For schedules and ticket information phone 615-974-5161.

Other local theaters include the *West Side Dinner Theatre,* Kingston Pike (615-966-6731), the *Laurel Theatre,* 1538 Laurel Avenue (615-523-7641), and the *Knoxville Area Theatre of the Deaf,* 139 Woodlawn Avenue (615-577-3559), which produces plays, mime, and sign interpretation for music and dance.

The *Knoxville Civic Auditorium and Coliseum,* 500 Church Avenue, S.E., presents stage plays in the 2,534-seat auditorium and such spectacles as "Holiday on Ice" in the 7,000-seat coliseum. 615-524-2703. The annual five-day *Crafts-*

man's Fair of the Southern Highlands is held at the auditorium beginning the third Tuesday in October. Write to Knoxvisit for information.

Cherokee Caverns, on Route 17, the Oak Ridge Highway, one of the many cave systems in eastern Tennessee, is open to the public all year. 615-693-2655.

LAUREL BLOOMERY This sleepy hamlet of fewer than 100 persons, on U.S. 91 in the very northeast corner of Tennessee, produces an elegant line of dinnerware marketed in more than six hundred retail stores across the United States and abroad. *Iron Mountain Stoneware* is one of only a few firms in the world producing contemporary high-fired stoneware. The extremely high temperatures at which this ceramic ware is fired make it ovenproof and chip-resistant. Each piece is hand-dipped and painted with decorative artwork. Tours of the plant are conducted on weekdays, and the pottery maintains a retail store where discount sales are held each year at Thanksgiving and Mother's Day. 615-727-8888.

MARYVILLE The seat of Blount County is named for Mary Grainger Blount, wife of Governor William Blount, for whom Blount County is named. *Sam Houston Schoolhouse (ca.* 1794), on Sam Houston Schoolhouse Road off Route 33, is the oldest original schoolhouse in Tennessee. In 1807, when he was fourteen years old, Sam Houston (1793–1863) came from Virginia to Blount County with his widowed mother. A restless young man, he spent three years living with the Cherokee and returned to teach in this country school in 1812. He charged $8 per pupil for a term that began after spring planting and ended with fall harvest. Rebuilt from original materials in 1954, the schoolhouse stands in a quiet glade, and the spring from which the students drank still flows. A soldier and statesman, Houston was a giant figure in the great era of American expansion: he was also a lawyer, an adopted Cherokee, a congressman, governor of Tennessee (1827–29), com-

At Iron Mountain Stoneware in Laurel Bloomery, each piece is dipped and painted with decorative artwork by hand.

In 1812 Sam Houston taught in this log schoolhouse near Maryville. Each pupil paid $8 tuition for a term that began after spring planting and ended at fall harvest.

mander in chief of the Texan army that routed Santa Anna at San Jacinto and achieved Texan independence; his name was given to the city of Houston; and he was twice President of Texas (1836–38 and 1841–44) and one of the first two Texas senators (1846–59). And yet Houston later said that as a teacher "I experienced a higher feeling of dignity and self-satisfaction than from any office or honor which I have since held." Open Tues.–Sat. 9 to dusk, Sun. 1 to dusk. Free.

MAYNARDVILLE *Big Ridge State Rustic Park,* on Route 61, includes 3,600 acres on the shores of Norris Lake, originally developed by the TVA as a demonstration park. It has a visitors' center, nature exhibits, 50 campsites, 19 cabins, and a group camp, as well as areas for swimming, fishing, boating, horseback riding, picnicking, and hiking. Write the park at Maynardville, TN 37807. 615-992-5523.

MORRISTOWN *David Crockett Tavern and Museum* is at the eastern edge of Morristown on U.S. 11E. Although tall tales exaggerated everything about him, creating a legendary character that sometimes obscured the man, Davy Crockett was real, one of the many truly picturesque men who peopled Tennessee in its early years. He was a bear hunter, Indian-fighter, raconteur, state legislator, and a three-term United States congressman. His own humor, wit, and engaging egotism probably gave birth to a few of the tallest of those tales. Sometime in the 1790s, his father, John Crockett, opened a small six-room tavern on the Abingdon-Knoxville Road near the present city of Morristown, and it was here that David spent his early years. In the 1950s, a re-creation of the original tavern was built near the site, using materials and furnishings taken from nearby surviving buildings of the same vintage. It is now a museum of items used and fashioned by early Tennessee pioneers. Open April 15 to November 1 Mon.–Sat. 9–5, Sun. 2–5. Nominal charge.

Panther Creek State Park, off U.S. 11E, 6 miles west of

Davy Crockett spent his early years in the tavern built by his father near Morristown in the 1790s. This replica was built on the site, using materials salvaged from other buildings of that vintage.

Davy Crockett was born in a cabin on a bank of the Nolichucky River near Limestone, east of Greeneville. This replica of his birthplace is part of Davy Crockett Birthplace Park.

Morristown, on the shore of Cherokee Lake, includes a visitors' center, a picnic area, bathhouses, and 50 developed campsites. Boats are available nearby. Write the park at P.O., Morristown, TN 37814. 615-581-2623.

NORRIS The *Museum of Appalachia,* 16 miles north of Knoxville, a mile off I-75, is a product of one man's lifelong respect for the common people of the mountains. "I hold the strong conviction that the true breed of diminishing mountain folk of Appalachia are among the most admirable people in the world. I have always loved these people even as a child," writes John Rice Irwin, creator and proprietor. For twenty years he has combed Appalachia collecting more than 200,000 pioneer relics, and with them he has lovingly created a complete and authentic vision of frontier Appalachian life—an entire village of thirty reconstructed and fully furnished log structures, with an operating farm, an exhibit barn, and a craft shop. Shingle-making, basket-making, apple butter-making, spinning, weaving, and other traditional skills are demonstrated on Sunday afternoons during the summer months. Among the village structures, many of them brought from elsewhere in the Appalachian region, are the *Arnwine Cabin,* included in the National Register of Historic Places as a genuine example of an early-nineteenth-century mountain home; the *McClung House,* a dog-trot house (so-called because of the passageway between the two main units) built in the 1790s; an early dirt-floored cabin chosen by CBS as the set of a Daniel Boone television series; and many shops, storehouses, and outbuildings. Open all year daily during daylight hours. Special tours and group rates by appointment. Nominal charge; children under six free. 615-494-7680.

Norris Dam State Resort Park, off U.S. 441, just north of Norris, is on Norris Lake, formed by Norris Dam, which was begun in 1933 as the first project of the newly created Tennessee Valley Authority. Some of the park's more than 2,000

Russ Rose and his wife, Nancy, make baskets from white oak splints at the Museum of Appalachia in Norris, where native craftsmen demonstrate traditional skills.

The McClung House, one of thirty reconstructed and fully furnished buildings at the Museum of Appalachia in Norris. This house, built in the 1790s, was used as a Civil War Sweetwater Valley near Knoxville in the 1790s, was used as a Civil War

acres are virgin forest, and there are several scenic overlooks. Facilities include a restaurant (open summer only), 45 cabins, a swimming pool, a craft shop, campgrounds, playgrounds, and summer naturalist and recreation programs. Opportunities abound for fishing, boating, and hiking. Free. Write the park at P.O., Norris, TN 37828. 615-426-7461.

At the park the *Will G. and Helen H. Lenoir Museum,* half a mile below Norris Dam on U.S. 441, contains a large collection of pioneer artifacts, primarily from the Appalachian region. A gristmill built in 1795 still grinds corn each summer day. Open daily 9–5 in summer; weekends only September through May Sat. 9–5, Sun. 1–5. Free.

OAK RIDGE   Between 1940 and 1945, the population of rural Anderson County nearly tripled. The new city of Oak Ridge was built in the Tennessee countryside as a home for the nation's first uranium purifying plant, part of the Manhattan Project. Until 1949, Oak Ridge was a secret city, fenced, gated, and closed to the public. On the day that Oak Ridge opened its gates, the American Museum of Atomic Energy also opened, to demonstrate the principles and worth of the work done at Oak Ridge. Now called the *American Museum of Science and Energy,* 300 Tulane Avenue, 15 minutes from I-40 and I-75, it has broadened its scope to portray solar and other power alternatives as well as nuclear energy. Models, movies, displays, and demonstrations tell the story of energy. Other activities include a children's film festival every Wednesday at 2:30 and an annual paper airplane contest. Open Mon.–Sat. 9–5, Sun. 12:30–5; summer until 6. Free. 615-576-3200.

The *X-10 Reactor* at the *Oak Ridge National Laboratory,* Bethel Valley Road, was the first full-scale nuclear reactor in the world (November 4, 1943), the first to produce significant amounts of heat energy and measurable amounts of plutonium 239, and the first reactor to produce radioactive isotopes for medical therapy. Dormant since 1963, it is now a

The graphite reactor at the Oak Ridge National Laboratory, the first full-scale nuclear reactor in the world, began operating on November 4, 1943, and was a prime producer of radioisotopes for twenty years. Removed from service in 1963, the reactor is now a National Historic Landmark.

The American Museum of Science and Energy at Oak Ridge portrays the potentials of nuclear, solar, geothermal, and traditional sources of energy and houses a pictorial history of the development of Oak Ridge during World War II.

Silver Dollar City at Pigeon Forge is a theme park built around a reconstructed 1870s mining town where authentic mountain crafts are demonstrated.

National Historic Landmark. Open Mon.–Sat. 9–4. Closed holidays. Free.

The *University of Tennessee Forestry Stations and Arboretum,* 901 Kerr Hollow Road, encompasses 250 acres of second-growth hardwood and pine forests traversed by 7.5 miles of roads and 2.5 miles of foot trails. Native plant associations and ecological relationships are emphasized in the California, Southern Coastal Plain, Central China, and Heath forest-association models. Plants from these and other regions are planted in natural associations on sites suited to their growth requirements. Major collections include pines, magnolias, dogwoods, holly, willows, and dwarf and unusual conifers. More than a thousand individual plants are now labeled. Annual activities include a fall arboretum walk. Open weekdays 8–5, weekends 8–5 in spring and fall. Free. 615-483-3571.

PIGEON FORGE   This town, 6 miles north of Gatlinburg on U.S. 441, is the site of several amusement areas.

Silver Dollar City is a theme park based on the pioneer heritage of the Smokies. The Mountain Music Festival in late June and early July and the National Crafts Festival in October are held here. Open daily April 9 through October 31: 10–6 from April 9 until May 29, 10–7 until June 26, 10–10 until July 19, 10–8 until August 23, 10–6 until October 31. Fee charged. Season passes available. 615-453-4616.

Magic World, on U.S. 441, is a fantasy amusement park with live magic shows, jugglers, and a dinosaur museum during the summer months. 615-453-8044.

The *Tommy Bartlett Water Circus,* on U.S. 441, is a boat, water-ski, and stage show on Lake Gatlinburg. Open May 20 through October. 615-453-9473.

The *Old Mill,* on the bank of the Little Pigeon River at the foot of the Great Smoky Mountains, was built in 1830 by William Love, whose family owned the iron forge for which the town is named. The mill, a reminder of an earlier way of

Plunging 256 feet into a shallow pool on the floor of a canyon, Fall Creek Falls is the highest waterfall in the eastern United States. Fall Creek Falls State Resort Park near Pikeville is the second-largest park in the Tennessee

life, has been in continuous operation since its construction and still grinds the meal for sale in its gift shop. Open Mon.–Sat. 8:30–6. Free. 615-453-4628.

The *Pigeon Forge Pottery,* near the mill, has been turning out handmade figures and utensils for decades. It is particularly noted for its whimsical figures of Smoky Mountains wildlife. Visitors may walk through the workrooms and watch the pottery being made, Mon.–Sat. 9–4. The showroom is open until 6. Free. 615-453-3883.

PIKEVILLE *Fall Creek Falls State Resort Park,* off Route 30, is the second largest park in the Tennessee system. It was named for a falls that drops 256 feet into the pool below. It comprises 16,000 acres and some of the most rugged scenery combined with some of the most civilized recreation facilities, including an inn and restaurant, an eighteen-hole golf course and pro shop, a lodge, craft shops, cabins and campsites, a nature center and lodge, playgrounds, an amphitheater, and a swimming pool. Write the park at Pikeville, TN 37367. 615-881-3241.

ROAN MOUNTAIN *Roan Mountain State Resort Park,* near the Tennessee–North Carolina border, off Route 143 south of the community of Roan Mountain, showcases hundreds of acres of spectacular scenery. When the rhododendron blooms in late June, this broad, grassy plateau, extending for 6 miles at an elevation near six thousand feet, becomes perhaps the supreme visual experience of the southern Appalachians. Elisha Mitchell, for whom Mount Mitchell, in North Carolina, was named, described Roan Mountain as "the most beautiful of all the high mountains . . . a vast meadow without a tree to obstruct this prospect, where a person may gallop his horse for a mile or two with Carolina at his feet on one side and Tennessee on the other, a green ocean of mountains rising in tremendous billows immediately around him." The park is relatively new and not yet completely developed, but there are picnic areas, campsites, and cross-country ski trails, and a Rhododendron Festival is held in late June. Write to Roan Mountain State Resort Park, Roan Mountain, TN 37687. 615-772-3303.

ROGERSVILLE The *Rogersville Historic District,* bounded by North Boyd, Kyle, Clinch, and North Bend streets, McKinney Avenue, and South Rogen Road, is a relatively undisturbed early-nineteenth-century neighborhood. Federal and Greek Revival buildings remain along tree-lined streets around a central square. The *Hawkins County Courthouse* is one of the oldest in Tennessee, and the *Hale Springs Hotel* was built in 1824 as a tavern for stage travelers. The first settlements in the area were made in 1772; Rogersville was laid out in 1787, and Knoxville's *Gazette,* one of the earliest newspapers in the state, began publication here in 1791.

RUGBY This nineteenth-century English colony was the personal inspiration of one man. Thomas Hughes, whose popular novel *Tom Brown's School Days* was an autobiographical account of his education in Rugby, England, was a social reformer who saw in America the solution to a dilemma created by the strict English class-system. The younger sons of English gentry were denied by law the inheritance of their fathers and denied by custom the opportunity to support themselves. Medicine, law, and the clergy, the only professions acceptable to their class, were overcrowded, and their parents, Hughes complained, "would rather see their sons starve like gentlemen than thrive in a trade or profession that is beneath them." In America, the land of the self-made man, Hughes believed these disenfranchised Englishmen could put their industry to use in farming and the trades without embarrassment, and their education to use in a cultivated village society after hours. The Rugby colony, named for Hughes's school, was founded October 5, 1880, amid worldwide attention, but suffered continual adversity through its first decade,

The Hughes Public Library, named for Thomas Hughes, the founder of the utopian community of Rugby, houses one of the finest collections of Victorian literature in America.

Christ Church Episcopal at Rugby is one of seventeen original buildings remaining from the utopian community founded in 1880 by author and social reformer Thomas Hughes.

including an outbreak of typhoid. As in most utopian communities, the reality proved harsher than the dream.

Today Rugby is a quiet community of perhaps a hundred residents, some the descendants of original colonists. Seventeen original buildings remain. The *Hughes Public Library* (1882) houses a priceless collection of Victorian literature. Weekly services are held in *Christ Church Episcopal* which retains its original hanging lamps and 1849 rosewood reed organ. *Kingstone Lisle,* the cottage built for Thomas Hughes, and *Twin Oaks,* one of the stateliest residences, are restored. A replica of *Percy Cottage,* another home, serves as a welcome center. Open March 1 through November 30 Mon.–Sat. 9–5, Sun. 12–5. Nominal charge; children under six free. Group rates and winter tours available by appointment. On the first weekend in August, the private homes of Rugby are opened to the public for the *Annual Rugby Pilgrimage.* Write the Rugby Restoration Association, P.O. Box 8, Highway 52, Rugby, TN 37733. 615-628-2441.

SEVIERVILLE   Sevierville, 14 miles north of Gatlinburg on U.S. 441, is the seat of Sevier County. Both town and county are named for the first governor of Tennessee, John Sevier, who concluded a treaty with the Indians in 1785 ceding the land south of the French Broad River, including what is now Sevier County, to the settlers. The *Sevier County Courthouse* on Court Avenue, completed in 1896, has been restored. An eclectic design, it features unusually extensive use of columns, pilasters, and arches and culminates in an elaborate central clock tower and cupola.

Forbidden Caverns, off U.S. 411, on Route 8 between Sevierville and Newport, the largest of several limestone caves near Sevierville, has a colorful history. Inhabited by Indians centuries ago, it was first explored by white men in 1919; in the 1930s and 1940s, moonshiners took advantage of the cave's isolation and its pure underground stream. Later, limestone was quarried here, and in 1967, the cave was opened to the public. The source of its water remains unknown, leading some scientists to imagine an underground lake yet to be revealed. One of the largest walls of precious onyx ever discovered gleams in the cave's artificial light. Open daily April 1 through October 31. Admission fee charged. 615-453-5972.

SWEETWATER The *Lost Sea* in *Craighead Caverns,* on U.S. 68, according to *The Guinness Book of Records* is the largest underground lake in the world. Fifty-five-minute conducted tours of the caverns include a walk through various rooms and halls and an excursion on the lake, where unusually large rainbow trout glide beneath the glass-bottomed boat. These caverns are among only a few in the world where anthodites, rare cave flowers, are found; there are as many on these walls as there are on the rest of the world's caves combined. The ancient history of the cave is suggested by the bones of a large Pleistocene jaguar discovered here and now in the American Museum of Natural History in New York. Casts of bones and tracks are on display at the visitors' center. Open daily 9 to sundown; closed Christmas day. Fee charged. 615-337-6616. Adjacent to the caverns, *Lost City* includes early Tennessee cabins, craft demonstrations, and a train ride.

TOWNSEND In an outdoor amphitheater surrounded by mountains, on Route 73, two biblical dramas are presented during the summer months. The *Smoky Mountain Passion Play* is a reenactment of the life of Christ by a forty-member cast. Performances at 8:45 Mon., Wed., and Fri., June 15 through August 24. The same cast presents *Damascus Road,* a series of biblical scenes including the death of Stephen and the conversion of Paul, 8:45 Tues., Thurs., and Sat. June 16 through August 26. Fee charged; group discounts. For reservations or tickets, write Smoky Mountain Passion Play, Townsend, TN 37882. 615-448-2244; before June 10, call 615-984-4111.

Tuckaleechee Caverns, off Route 73, offers tours every half hour. Open daily 9–7 summer, 9–6 spring and fall; closed November through March. Admission fee. 615-448-2274.

From Townsend it is a short drive to *Cades Cove* in the Great Smoky Mountains National Park, a 3,000-acre valley where a pioneer settlement is re-created, including a century-old water-powered gristmill.

VONORE *Fort Loudon* is on the Tennessee River off U.S. 411, south of the Little Tennessee River Bridge near Vonore. During the French and Indian War, in 1756–57, British South Carolina erected this fort in Cherokee country to impede French penetration into the Mississippi Valley and to cement its uneasy alliance with the Cherokee in the west. Diamond-shaped, with a bastion at each corner, it was closer in design and construction to European forts of the period than to its counterparts on the American frontier. By the spring of 1760 the Cherokee, who had solicited this first English garrison in what is now Tennessee, had become alienated by British maltreatment and besieged the fort for five months. The garrison finally surrendered under terms guaranteeing their safe withdrawal; however, a day's march from the fort, the Cherokee massacred more than a score of the evacuating party. The fort, subsequently burned, was never regarrisoned. It now has been reconstructed to its 1760 appearance, as determined by careful historical and archeological research. Open daily 9–5:30. Nominal charge.

WARTBURG *Frozen Head Natural Area,* about 6 miles northeast of Wartburg on Route 62, is a 10,000-acre wilderness with more than 50 miles of backpacking and day-hike trails. Future plans include a nature center with a laboratory, a library, and classroom facilities, a group lodge, and primitive campsites; development and disturbance to the ecology will be kept to a minimum to preserve the value of the area for environmental study. Write the State Natural Area, Wartburg, TN 37887. 615-346-3318.

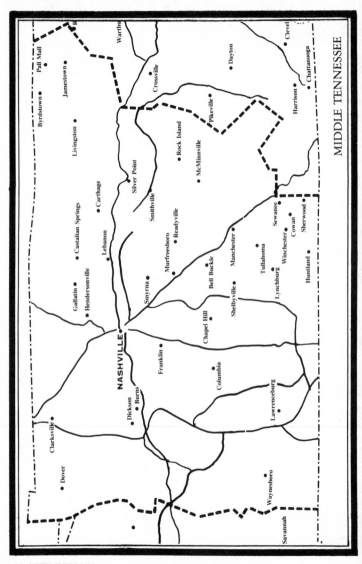

MIDDLE TENNESSEE

MIDDLE TENNESSEE

Middle Tennessee, circumscribed by the broad loop of the Tennessee River, includes roughly half of Tennessee. In the east, it begins where the land rises steeply up out of the great valley of the Tennessee River onto the Cumberland Plateau, the rolling upland region known to early settlers as the "Wilderness" because of its few inhabitants and its poor agricultural prospects. In more recent years the plateau has yielded coal, as well as sandstone and other minerals. Two more of Tennessee's six physiographic regions lie in Middle Tennessee west of the plateau: the highland rim and the central basin. The rim, the largest of the state's regions, encircles the basin and is on sedimentary rock, chiefly shale and limestone, which has, in places, been eroded by underground water to form sinkholes and caverns. The rim's southern counties produce cotton, and in its northern counties tobacco is the principal crop. In his analysis of Tennessee's resources written in the late nineteenth century Joseph Killebrew describes the central basin as the "bottom of an oval dish, of which the Highlands form the broad, flat brim," and pronounces it the "center of wealth and political influence and rich in all the elements of a splendid civilization." Early settlers, having struggled across the harsh plateau, found the basin a green and fruitful land capable of supporting crops. Its fertile limestone soil much resembles that in the bluegrass region of

Kentucky, and its lush pasturage is the turf of the Tennessee walking horse.

Pastoral beauty, the homes of renowned Tennesseans from Andrew Jackson's stately Hermitage to Alvin York's humble farm and gristmill, national military parks, limestone caverns, ancient Indian ruins, the Natchez Trace Parkway, the oldest registered distillery in the United States, museums of art, history, railroading, and religion, and the myriad attractions of Nashville, Tennessee's capital, are all found in Middle Tennessee.

BELL BUCKLE   In 1870, William R. Webb founded the *Webb School* in Culleoka. In 1886, he moved his school to Bell Buckle because the saloonkeepers of Culleoka offended his temperance beliefs by plying his students with whiskey. The *Junior Room,* built that first year in Bell Buckle, is preserved as it was in the nineteenth century, with school paraphernalia and the pot-bellied stove that warmed it in winter. The sole improvement has been the introduction of electric lights. In this small wood-shingled and clapboarded one-room schoolhouse, "Old Sawney," as his pupils called him, established a preparatory school whose graduates were welcomed in the finest universities; the governors of three states and ten Rhodes Scholars studied in this humble classroom. An annual art and craft festival is held on the campus in late October. Open daily 8–4. Free. 615-389-9322.

BURNS   *Montgomery Bell State Resort Park* is off U.S. 70. On this site, Montgomery Bell's ironworks molded the cannonballs used by Andrew Jackson's artillery at the Battle of New Orleans. In 1810, the Reverend Samuel McAdoo, a Presbyterian minister active in the Great Revival of 1800, founded the Cumberland Presbyterian Church at his home here. An inn and restaurant, cabins, picnic areas, 110 campsites, horseback riding, swimming, fishing, boating, hiking trails, and a group camp. Write the park at Box 684, Burns, TN 37029. 615-797-3101.

BYRDSTOWN The *Cordell Hull Birthplace* is on Route 42, about 1½ miles southwest of Byrdstown. Statesman Cordell Hull was born on October 2, 1871, in this log cabin in the foothills of the Cumberland Mountains. His career included terms in the Tennessee General Assembly, the United States House of Representatives, the Senate, and more than a decade (1933–44) as Secretary of State, during which he worked to lay the groundwork for the creation of the United Nations. Largely for this effort, he was awarded the Nobel Peace Prize at the culmination of his career. Open daily 10–6 May 28 through Labor Day. Free.

CARTHAGE *Cordell Hull Lake,* a project of the U.S. Army Corps of Engineers, is surrounded by land reserved for outdoor recreation. From Carthage, take Route 85 north to the town of Defeated and follow the signs to the Defeated Creek Recreation Area. Twenty-two miles of horseback riding trails vary from gentle grades to precipitous paths along the steep bluffs overlooking the river. The *Bearwaller Gap Hiking Trail,* named for the depressions where black bears once "wallered" to cool themselves, winds 6 miles through cedar glades and, on the higher elevations, through oak, hickory, and associated hardwoods. The cold waters of the lake harbor trout, and the Roaring River section is suited for canoeing. 615-735-2244.

CASTALIAN SPRINGS This is one of the oldest settlements in Middle Tennessee. In 1772 Isaac Bledsoe, a hunter and explorer from southwestern Virginia, came upon a salt lick here surrounded by so many buffalo that he was afraid to dismount for fear of being trampled. In 1783 he returned with his family and built a stockaded fort on a hill overlooking the springs. His brother and later Isaac himself were killed by Indians, but the village continued to grow. In

1828 A. R. Wynne, William Cage, and Stephen Roberts built *Wynnewood,* on Route 25 (Gallatin-Hartsville Pike) in Castalian Springs, 9 miles east of Gallatin, a handsome stagecoach inn and mineral-springs resort. Later, as sole proprietor, Wynne built cottages on the east lawn and a racecourse near the creek. Andrew Jackson, a friend and frequent visitor, often brought a favorite Thoroughbred to race against one from Wynne's stable. The estate remained in the family until 1971, when the grandson of the builder conveyed it to the state. Wynnewood may have been the largest log building ever erected in Tennessee (it is the largest to have survived); yet it remains a testament to the simple harmony of log construction. The main house is 142 feet long with an open hallway, or dogtrot, through the center. The logs, most of them oak and some as long as 32 feet, are set firmly on a stone foundation. All rooms have outside doors, opening onto the gallery that extends 110 feet across the rear of the building. The attached kitchen is constructed of black walnut logs. Open April 1 through October 31 Wed.–Sat. 10–4, Sun. 1–5; winter months by appointment. Nominal charge.

CHAPEL HILL *Henry Horton State Park* is on the estate of Henry H. Horton, the thirty-sixth governor of Tennessee, on the banks of the Duck River. It is primarily a golfing resort but also has picnic areas, a skeet and trap range, lighted tennis courts, riding trails, and a swimming pool, as well as cabins, a 72-room resort inn, 90 campsites, and a restaurant. Write the park at Chapel Hill, TN 37034. 615-364-2222.

CLARKSVILLE On a peninsula at the confluence of the Cumberland and Red rivers, Clarksville was founded in 1784 and named for Colonel George Rogers Clark (1752–1818), leader of successful Revolutionary War campaigns against the British and Indians in the Northwest. The area has long been known by the reputation of its dark-fired, fire-cured rather than air-cured, tobacco. Allen Tate—who with

John Crowe Ransom, Robert Penn Warren, and several other poets and critics founded the literary magazine the *Fugitive* at Vanderbilt University in the 1920s—and Tate's wife, Caroline Gordon, lived for many years in Clarksville. Tate's *The Fathers* (1938) is a superior novel of the Civil War, and Gordon wrote several novels set around Clarksville in the Cumberland River region. Among the surviving buildings of historical interest are the *Clarksville Federal Building* (1897–98), Commerce and South Second streets; *Emerald Hill* (Eagle's Nest) (1830s), North Second Street, the nineteenth-century home of Gustavus A. Henry, renowned political orator and senator in the Confederate Congress; and the *Sevier Station* (1792–94), on the west side of Walker Street below B Street, a limestone stronghouse built by Valentine Sevier for protection against Indians and the site in 1794 of one of the territory's worst massacres. After the massacre, Valentine wrote his brother John Sevier, saying that his son had been killed and his daughter scalped and describing the attack, "Such a scene no man ever witnessed before. Nothing but screams and the roaring of guns . . ." A walking tour of downtown Clarksville and a longer trail reaching nearby landmarks of local history have been planned by local historians. Write Clarksville Area Chamber of Commerce, 312 Madison Street, P.O. Box 883, Clarksville, TN 37040. 615-647-2331.

Austin Peay State University, bordering College Street, was named for the governor of Tennessee (1923-27), and is the site each April of the State of Tennessee Old Time Fiddler's Championship.

About 30 miles west of Clarksville via U.S. 79 is the southern entrance to *Land Between the Lakes,* a 175,000-acre peninsula being developed by the Tennessee Valley Authority as a national demonstration in outdoor recreation, environmental education, and resource management. Nestled between Kentucky Lake (the Tennessee River) on the west and

Lake Barkley (the Cumberland River) on the east, this preserve, 8 miles wide and 40 miles long, has a multitude of special areas created to invite camping, fishing, hunting, boating, and picnicking. Although the outer shores of both lakes are lined with marinas and a state resort park is near each of the four entrances to the peninsula, there are no commercial establishments within the Land Between the Lakes. There are 3,500 miles of shoreline, more than 300 miles of backcountry roads, more than 200 miles of hiking trails, and canoe, bicycle, and riding trails. More than 800 campsites are available in three full-service family campgrounds. The 5,000-acre *Environmental Education Center* includes the Center Station, where films and displays orient the visitor; Center Furnace, which recalls the iron industry that once flourished here; Empire Farm, where children can see domestic animals and old farm furnishings; Youth Station, an outdoor school; Silo Overlook, a panorama of Lake Barkley; and nature trails, including a paved trail accessible to the physically handicapped. Hiking trails include the 56-mile North-South Trail and the Fort Henry Hiking Trails, which follow the route of General Ulysses S. Grant from Fort Henry to Fort Donelson. Canoeists will enjoy the Little River Canoe Trail. More than two thousand acres are set aside for off-road vehicles, and there is a wrangler's camp for horseback riders. The *Homeplace-1850* is a living-history farm. The most remarkable sight in the park is the herd of buffalo (American bison) that roams a 200-acre pasture alongside the Trace, the north-south highway. In winter months bald and golden eagles inhabit quiet coves. The central information office is just off U.S. 68 near the center of the park. To enter from Tennessee, turn north on Route 49 just west of Dover and continue a short distance to the information station. Write Information Office, Land Between the Lakes, Tennessee Valley Authority, Golden Pond, KY 42231. 502-924-5602 or 502-362-8367.

Dunbar Cave State Natural Area, off Route 13, 3 miles northeast of Clarksville, is a 110-acre natural area that includes a cave once owned by country music performer Roy Acuff. During the 1940s and 1950s, it was operated commercially, and the surrounding site was an amusement park. Stars of the "Grand Ole Opry" attended square dances held in the mouth of the cave. The cave is now closed. Write the area at P.O. Box 580, Route 10, Clarksville, TN 37040. 615-645-9456.

COLUMBIA One block from the courthouse in Columbia is the *Ancestral Home of President James K. Polk,* 301 West Seventh Street, built in 1816 by Samuel Polk, father of our eleventh President. It is one of the earliest brick houses in Middle Tennessee. Among the memorabilia from Polk's career are portraits of him as a congressman and later as President, the Bible on which he swore his inaugural oath, and many personal items used in the White House. A daguerrotype of the President and his cabinet may be the earliest known photograph of the interior of the White House. Adjoining is the *Sisters' House,* home of Polk's two sisters and their families, built in 1820. The gardens include plantings of English boxwood, an herb garden, and a wildflower garden. The properties have recently undergone a three-year program to restore their nineteenth-century appearance. Open April through October Mon.–Sat. 9–5, November through March Mon.–Sat. 9–4, Sun. 1–5 all year. Nominal charge; group rates available. 615-388-2354.

The *Athenaeum* (1838), 808 Athenaeum Place, is the last remaining building of the Columbia Athenaeum, a private school founded by the Reverend Franklin Gillette Smith that trained thousands of women between 1852 and 1903. The building itself is Gothic Revival, with unusual Moorish arches that add an exotic aspect. Open Mon.–Sat. 9–4:30, Sun. 1–4:30. Admission fee charged.

The Columbia home of James K. Polk—who, as the eleventh president of the United States, approved the acquisition of Texas, California, and New Mexico—was altered in the late nineteenth century and early 1900s, but it has recently been restored to appear as it did before Polk's death in 1849.

COWAN   On the edge of the western escarpment of the Cumberland Plateau, Cowan came into being because of a railroad. Between 1848 and 1852, the Nashville and Chattanooga Railroad accomplished a remarkable engineering feat: the tunnel that was cut through Cumberland Mountain near Cowan, which was the site of a depot and railroad yard for pusher engines. The *Cowan Railroad Museum* commemorates the tunnel, the tradition of railroading in the Tennessee mountains, and the early history of the town. Housed in the Cowan Depot built in 1904, it contains railroading memorabilia, books, and a model-train room with a working scene of Cumberland Mountain. A steam engine and caboose sit in a landscaped park adjacent to the museum. Open daily April 1 through October 31 10–4, or by special request. Free; donations accepted. 615-967-7546.

DICKSON   In the late nineteenth century, followers of English author, art critic, and social theorist John Ruskin (1819–1900), who railed against the inequities of Victorian capitalism, founded a socialist colony near *Ruskin Cave* in Middle Tennessee. The self-supporting living experiment disbanded in 1899, but ruins of the settlement remain, and the ground-level cave, 10 miles north of Dickson on Yellow Creek Road (Erin Road), is open to the public. Open during summer, other seasons by appointment. Admission fee charged. 615-763-2850. Just ¼ mile away, on Yellow Creek Road, is *Jewel Cave,* where prehistoric bear bones 25,000 years old have been unearthed. First discovered in 1895, the cave has been open to the public since 1898. Guided tours, averaging one hour, are conducted all year. Admission fee charged. 615-763-2894.

DOVER   *Fort Donelson National Military Park,* on U.S. 79 in west Dover, was the scene, in February 1862, of one of the first decisive battles of the Civil War. The capture of Confederate Fort Donelson was the first major victory of Union

General Ulysses S. Grant; it enhanced his military reputation and reassured skeptical Union supporters. With the collapse of Fort Henry on the Tennessee River, the surrender of Fort Donelson on the Cumberland River led to eventual Union control of the Mississippi Valley and opened the South to invasion. It was here that Grant issued the ultimatum that eventually became his nickname: "unconditional surrender." At the park entrance the visitors' center contains a museum and an auditorium for an audio-visual display explaining the battle. The park includes a large portion of the battlefield, with remains of the earthen fort and perimeter earthworks. Replicas of two garrison cabins stand within the fort's walls, and artillery pieces representative of the original armaments are mounted on the earthworks. Tablets along a 10-mile tour route describe troop movements and encounters. During the warm months, particularly on weekends, demonstrations of period life are given by the staff. Open daily 8–4. Free. 615-232-5348.

The *Cross Creeks National Wildlife Refuge* headquarters is 3.5 miles southeast of Dover off Route 49. An intensive waterfowl-management program has attracted large numbers of ducks and Canada geese to this 8,861-acre refuge. Public fishing is permitted. Write the refuge at Box 113B, Dover, TN 37058.

FRANKLIN Less than 20 miles south of Nashville on U.S. 31 is the historic town of Franklin, where Andrew Jackson met the Chickasaw Indians to sign a peace treaty that lasted more than one hundred years, and where noted jurist John Marshall, John Eaton, the secretary of war under Andrew Jackson, and Thomas Hart Benton, later a Missouri senator, all practiced law. In Franklin and surrounding Williamson County, five Civil War battles were fought, including the bloody Battle of Franklin. On the afternoon of November 30, 1864, enraged because Union General John Schofield had slipped 22,000 Union troops and a supply train past his sleeping men along the Columbia Pike, Confederate General John B. Hood charged Union entrenchments in the south part of town, where houses, a school, and an industrial park now stand just off Columbia Avenue at Battle Avenue. Union casualties were 2,326; Confederate casualties exceeded 6,000, including 6 generals slain. These losses precipitated the final defeat of Hood's campaign two and a half weeks later in Nashville. Before the Civil War, the area including Franklin was one of the richest in Tennessee. In 1813, the oldest weekly newspaper in Tennessee, *The Review Appeal,* was established in Franklin. The area's slow recovery after the Civil War was based on tobacco cultivation for nearly a century.

Laid out in 1787, Franklin has many surviving nineteenth-century buildings. The entire original fifteen-block section centered around Main Street (Route 96) and Third Avenue (U.S. 31) is included in the National Register of Historic Places as the *Franklin Historic District.* A map and walking guide to more than twenty Federal, Greek Revival, and late-nineteenth-century structures is available from the Williamson County Chamber of Commerce, P.O. Box 156, Franklin, TN 37064, at 612 Main Street.

Similar information is to be had at the *Visitors Information Center* on Main Street northeast of the town square, housed in the *McPhail Office* in the Harpeth Mall complex. Once a doctor's office, this tiny example of antebellum architecture, built around 1813, is restored and is staffed daily by volunteers. Below are several of the many buildings in the town itself of historical or architectural interest. The homes, unless noted, are private, although several welcome visitors during the candlelight tour in early December.

The *Williamson County Courthouse* (1859), on the south corner of the square, one of the few remaining antebellum, small-town courthouses in the state, is built in the typical

Greek Revival style. The four columns are of locally mined cast iron. In the nineteenth century, severe frontier justice was meted out in the square with whippings, brandings, and confinement to stocks.

The *Confederate Monument* in the square, an Italian marble statue of a Confederate infantryman at parade rest, was erected in 1899 by the United Daughters of the Confederacy.

The *Eaton House* (*ca.* 1805), on Third Avenue northwest of the square, is a classical Federal house and one of the oldest dwellings in Franklin; it is known as the home of Elizabeth Eaton, whose son, John H. Eaton, served as secretary of war in the cabinet of his friend Andrew Jackson. Jackson stood by Eaton when Washington society rebuffed his wife, Peggy O'Neill, the daughter of an innkeeper, and the incident resulted in the resignation of several cabinet members and a long-standing feud between Jackson and his vice-president, John C. Calhoun.

The *Hiram Masonic Lodge* (1823), Second Avenue South, was the first Masonic lodge in Tennessee, chartered in 1809. The first Protestant Episcopal Church in Tennessee was organized here in 1827. At the time of its construction, this three-story brick building was said to be the tallest in Tennessee.

The *Old Factory Store,* East Main Street, is one of the oldest remaining buildings. As early as 1821, a large cotton factory was located next door, and the woolen and cotton cloth was sold in this store. It was later the shop of a hatter, a bank, and a temporary military hospital following the Battle of Franklin. The factory has been razed, and the store now houses a restaurant.

Saint Paul's Episcopal Church (1831–34), 510 Main Street, is the oldest Protestant Episcopal church in Tennessee. Damaged severely during the Civil War, when it was used as a hospital and its furnishings were broken up for firewood, it was later remodeled; Tiffany windows were added in 1915, and it is now among the most beautiful buildings in Franklin.

On Main Street is the *First Presbyterian Church,* built in 1907 to replace an earlier building that had occupied the site since 1842.

On Second Avenue is *Saint Philip's Catholic Church,* built in 1871 of bricks made and fired on the site. *Clouston Hall,* the home of a prominent Franklin physician, was built in the 1830s. The *Eelbeck House* was built in the traditional style of the early nineteenth century by a prosperous carriage-maker.

On Third Avenue is the *Marshall House,* built before 1805 to serve as both a home and school. The *Blackburn-Ewin House* was built in 1874 by John W. Blackburn, who personally chose each piece of lumber. The *White-Proctor House* is an 1870s structure with a pretty stairway. The *First Baptist Church* was built in the 1890s to replace an earlier church destroyed by fire. The *Moran-Pope House,* built in the 1820s, was the home and workshop of cabinetmaker Charles Moran, who created furniture for many of the finest Tennessee homes, including the Hermitage (see NASHVILLE). The *Knight-Mosley* House, a handsome residence, the earliest part of which is thought to have been built in the early nineteenth century, is distinguished by arched French windows, arched side panels, and a fanlight over the front door. The mistress of *Gaut House,* Sallie Ewin Gaut, used a trapdoor in the roof to spy on Union activities in Franklin during the Civil War. The *Cochrane-DeBrohun House,* built in the 1820s, sheltered many Franklin families during the Battle of Franklin. The *Eggleston House,* built in the 1880s, was the scene of a series of children's books written in the 1930s. The books about "Those Plummer Children," written by Christine Noble Govan, were inspired by the Eggleston children and this house, with its gazebo and latticed porch.

On Fourth Avenue, the *Walker-Ridley House,* built in the mid-nineteenth century, was later the home of Rogers

Caldwell, a financial baron reputed to be the richest man in the South in the 1920s. He moved here after losing his fortune in the Crash of 1929 and every Saturday until his death entertained the leading businessmen in Middle Tennessee to discuss world affairs and financial matters. The *Walker-Haliburton House* is one of three adjacent houses built in the mid-nineteenth century by Silas Walker. The *Bennett-Garrett House* was built in the 1870s by Walter James Bennett, a Confederate veteran and local businessman. The *Fourth Avenue Church of Christ,* first built in 1852 and heavily damaged in the Civil War, has been rebuilt several times since.

The *Carter House* (1830), on Columbia Avenue, was a Union command post during the Battle of Franklin, and the farm office claims the curious distinction of being the most bullet-ridden building surviving from the Civil War. In the basement where the Carter family huddled in terror as the battle raged around the house from dusk until after midnight, the Association for the Preservation of Tennessee Antiquities (APTA) maintains a museum of Civil War artifacts. Open Mon.–Sat. 9–4, Sun. 2–4. Nominal charge. 615-794-1733.

Carnton (ca. 1825), on Confederate Cemetery Drive, was built by Randall McGavock, member of a prominent Virginia family and one of the first settlers in this area. Once known for its elegant gardens, Carnton was used as a hospital after the Battle of Franklin. Five Confederate generals slain in the fighting were brought here; nearly fifteen hundred soldiers are buried in the adjoining cemetery.

From *Winstead Hill,* a knoll 2 miles south of town, General John B. Hood surveyed Union positions in Franklin and planned his disastrous attack. A large bronze relief map shows troop positions and movements during the battle.

Fort Granger (1863), off Liberty Pike, was built by Union forces and used for 2½ years to bombard Franklin and to control troop movements north to Nashville. Remains of trenches, gun emplacements, and walls are discernible. The fort has been purchased by the city, excavated for artifacts, and may become a park.

Carter's Court, across Columbia Avenue (U.S. 31) from the Carter House, is a quaint shopping development that includes the *Battle-O-Rama,* a three-dimensional multimedia re-creation of the Battle of Franklin. Open Mon.–Sat. 10–4:30, Sun. 12–4. Nominal charge.

GALLATIN Established in 1802, Gallatin was named for Albert Gallatin (1761–1849), the Swiss-born secretary of the treasury under presidents Jefferson and Madison (1801–14), who, incidental to his career as a statesman, wrote *Synopsis of the Indian Tribes . . . of North America* (1836) and founded the American Ethnological Society (1842).

Cragfont (1798) 5 miles east of Gallatin on Route 25, was the home of General James Winchester, first speaker of the Tennessee senate and a founder of Memphis, who came to Tennessee in 1787 to claim the land granted him for his service in the Revolutionary War. He brought stonemasons and ship's carpenters from his native Maryland to build Cragfont, which, though it is largely unadorned on the exterior, was for its period extraordinarily elegant in its furnishings, grounds, and second-floor ballroom. Built at a time when log construction was only beginning to give way to the use of abundant local brick and stone, Cragfont is significant in this transition for its use of locally quarried limestone and for the Spanish influence evident in the two-story galleries that flank the rear ell. Andrew Jackson and John Overton, Winchester's partners in planning Memphis, often visited at Cragfont. The house is furnished with Federal antiques; in the basement are a typical weaving room, a wine cellar, and a collection of early-nineteenth-century tools. Open April 15 through November 1 Tues.–Sat. 10–5, Sun. 1–6. Winter months by appointment. Nominal charge. Write Cragfont, Route 1, Box 42, Castalian Springs, TN 37031. 615-452-7070.

Bledsoe Creek State Camping Park, on Route 25, provides

133 developed campsites on a 164-acre site on the Bledsoe Creek Embayment of Old Hickory Lake. An environmental education area is planned for the future. Write the park at Route 2, Gallatin, TN 37066. 615-452-3706.

HENDERSONVILLE *Rock Castle* (1784–91), on Indian Road Southeast of Hendersonville, was built by Daniel Smith on land granted to him for his Revolutionary War service. Smith was appointed secretary of the Territory of the United States South of the River Ohio in 1790, later served as chairman of the committee to draft the Tennessee constitution, and in 1798 succeeded Andrew Jackson in the U.S. Senate. The two and a half–story limestone house is one of the oldest and finest examples of Federal architecture in Tennessee. Greek Revival additions were made in the 1850s, and much of the original woodwork and flooring remains. The house and grounds may be visited Tues.–Sat. 10–4, Sun. 1–4 spring through fall. Nominal charge. 615-824-0502.

HUNTLAND *Falls Mill,* a mile off U.S. 64, at Old Salem Crossroads, is a two and a half–story brick mill, built in 1873, that survives in a lovely and tranquil setting. The mill, restored in 1970, was originally a woolen mill and later a cotton mill, and itself succeeded an earlier mill on the site. The 1907 metal overshot waterwheel is 34 feet in diameter, one of the largest of its type. A country store occupies the second floor. Open all year. Free.

JAMESTOWN *Picket State Rustic Park,* approximately 20 miles northeast of Jamestown on Route 154 at the Kentucky border in a remote region of the Cumberland Mountains, contains a variety of interesting geological formations. It offers chalet cabins, a group camp, hiking, fishing, birdwatching, an abundance of wildlife and flora, and caves for exploring. A scenic trail leads to the nearby home and gristmill of Sergeant Alvin York. (See PALL MALL.) Write Picket State Rustic Park, Jamestown, TN 38556. 615-879-7017.

LAWRENCEBURG *David Crockett State Park,* off U.S. 64 northwest of Lawrenceburg, is on the banks of Shoal Creek, where Davy Crockett operated a powder mill, gristmill, and distillery around 1819. A gristmill has been reconstructed near the original site. From 1817 to 1822, Crockett lived in Lawrenceburg while serving in the Tennessee legislature. Facilities include 100 developed campsites, primitive camping areas, lighted tennis courts, a swimming pool, and a restaurant open all year, as well as fishing, boating, and picnicking. Write the park at P.O., Lawrenceburg, TN 38464. 615-762-9408.

LEBANON Named for the Biblical Lebanon because of its abundance of cedars, the town was a center of culture in antebellum Tennessee. *Cumberland College,* founded in 1842, counts among its graduates Cordell Hull (see also BYRDS-TOWN). On the campus of the *Castle Heights Military Academy,* on West Main, is the *Mitchell Mansion,* a stone Greek Revival structure with a two-story Corinthian portico flanked by single-story porches. Visitors are welcome weekdays; inquire at the front office.

Cedars of Lebanon State Day Use Park, on U.S. 231 and Route 10, preserves one of the largest remaining forests of red cedar in the United States. It has a visitors' center, 166 campsites, lodge, nature trails, and other recreational facilities. Write the park at Lebanon, TN 37087. 615-444-9394.

LIVINGSTON Historic buildings open to the public include the *Overton County Courthouse,* completed in 1869 and recently refurbished, and the *Governor Roberts Law Office,* on University Street, which contains books, documents, and personal items from the years 1880–1921.

Standing Stone State Rustic Park, on Route 52 between Livingston and Celina, consists of almost 11,000 acres on the vast Cumberland Plateau, extending from New York to Alabama, which impeded western migration and settlement in the eighteenth century. The park is the result of extensive reforestation efforts in the 1930s and is now distinguished by its woodlands, spring wildflowers, and natural diversity. At the park are rustic cabins, timberlodges, a seasonal restaurant, a swimming pool, a lodge, 50 tent and trailer campsites, group lodges, and a group camp. Write the Superintendent's Office, Livingston, TN 38570. 615-823-6347.

Dale Hollow Lake, north of Livingston, was the source of a recent world-record smallmouth bass. On the Highland rim section of northern Tennessee and southern Kentucky, Dale Hollow is surrounded by forests, and its water is clear enough to invite scuba diving. Immediately below the dam is a national fish hatchery open to the public. Follow signs from Celina. Write to the U.S. Army Engineer District, P.O. Box 1070, Nashville, TN 37202.

LYNCHBURG Nestled in the foothills of the Cumberland Mountains, the small town of Lynchburg surrounds an eighteenth-century square that is all but unchanged. Atop the most prominent of the encircling hills stand several enormous barrelhouses of the *Jack Daniel Distillery,* the town's industry and reason for being—and the second largest taxpayer in Tennessee (the first being a snuff manufactory in Memphis). The distillery, the oldest registered one in the United States, offers extensive visitor tours daily. The carefully orchestrated tour begins with a climb up outside stairs to the upper level of the barrelhouses, in which a slide show depicts the Jack Daniel's method of making sour mash whiskey. Oriented, the visitor is taken by minibus to an overlook from which he views the charcoal-making facility. The tour continues on foot to the limestone cave from which springwater has flowed into the making of Jack Daniel's for more than 150 years; to the original frame office where Jasper ("Jack") Newton Daniel conducted his business until his death in 1911; to the still house where the mash of corn, rye, and barley malt is cooked and fermented; and to the charcoal-mellowing build-ing, where the new whiskey is dripped to seep slowly down through 12 feet of charcoal enroute to U.S. Government re-ceiving cisterns. After a stop at the bottling plant, the tour concludes at the starting point, where lemonade is served (the county is dry) and descriptive literature distributed. Free. 615-759-4221.

McMINNVILLE *Cumberland Caverns,* 7 miles south-east of McMinnville on Route 8, are labyrinthine caves first discovered in 1810 and mined for saltpeter during the wars of 1812 and 1861. Their vast extent was not realized until 1948, and today many miles of winding passages have been mapped. Guided tours daily 9–5 June through August; weekends only May, September and October. By appointment November through April. Fee charged. 615-668-4396.

MANCHESTER *Old Stone Fort State Archaeological Ar-ea* is about 1.5 miles west of Manchester, just off U.S. 41. The ancient walled structure for which this park is named was built, probably between A.D. 30 and 430, by Indians of the Middle Woodland Period, and most archeologists believe that the series of rock and earthen walls was built for ceremonial purposes. But because the embankments, which enclose about 50 acres, occupy a natural defense position on the bluffs overlooking the forks of the Duck River, they continue to be referred to as a fort. The river tumbles through a beauti-ful waterfall, and there are large stands of mountain laurel. Park facilities include 50 campsites, picnic sites, hiking trails, and a visitors' center and museum that depicts the colorful legends surrounding the origins of the fort. Tours are con-ducted by a park naturalist during the summer months. The park is open all year daily 8 A.M. to 10 P.M. in summer; 8 A.M. to sundown in winter. Write the Superintendent's Office, Manchester, TN 37355. 615-728-0751.

MURFREESBORO Murfreesboro was the capital of

Tennessee from 1819 to 1825. Its original name was Cannonsburg, for Newton Cannon, governor of Tennessee from 1835 to 1839. When Cannon's popularity waned, the town's name was changed to honor Colonel Hardy Murfree, a Revolutionary War veteran and father of the first mistress of Oaklands. When the courthouse burned in 1822, the state legislature moved to the Masonic Hall, but in 1825 the delegates moved to Nashville in search of a more suitable hall. The *Rutherford County Courthouse* (1859) occupies the site of that original courthouse on the public square at the heart of the town. During the Civil War the courthouse was occupied by Union troops and recaptured by General Nathan Bedford Forrest, July 13, 1862.

Stones River National Battlefield and Cemetery is in the northwestern corner of Murfreesboro. On the banks of the Stones River along the Nashville Pike, a pivotal Civil War battle took place in the struggle for the rich farmlands of Middle Tennessee. From dawn on December 31, 1862, until late afternoon of January 2, 1863, Union forces under Major General William Rosecrans beat back the repeated attacks of Confederate troops under General Braxton Bragg. Rosecrans was actually the pursuer, having followed Bragg south from Kentucky. Although both armies claimed victory and both suffered almost equally vicious losses, when the smoke cleared, the Union army was the sole possessor of Murfreesboro, with control of the transportation axis running southeastward through Tennessee. The battlefield today appears much as it did in 1863. The visitors' center includes a museum and a color-slide presentation on the battle. Visitors may take a self-guided tour of the field or a one-hour automobile tape-tour that includes a first-person account. There are also hiking and bicycling trails and picnic tables. During the summer months, artillery is demonstrated with live projectiles that explode down-range. Demonstrations are Fri., Sat. and

Losses to both armies were heavy in the fighting at Stones River on the last day of 1862 and the first days of 1863. The bitterly contested ground is now Stones River National Battlefield and Cemetery at Murfreesboro.

Oaklands, at Murfreesboro, has been restored to its 1865 appearance. It was owned by a physician in the last century, and a museum on the grounds displays early medical instruments.

Sun. 1:30 and 3:30 mid-June through the third week in August. The park is open daily, except Christmas, 8–5 with extended hours in summer. Free. 615-893-9501.

Fortress Rosecrans Site is west of Murfreesboro at Stones River. After the battle at Stones River, Rosecrans occupied Murfreesboro and constructed the largest earthwork fort built by the Union during the Civil War. It originally covered more than 200 acres, and from the huge supply-base within it, the Union army launched a successful attack on the Confederate rail center in Chattanooga and drove the wedge through the Confederacy that led ultimately to the capture of Atlanta and Sherman's march to the sea. Several hundred yards of earthworks remain, averaging 15 feet in height.

Oaklands, on North Maney Avenue, is built on Revolutionary War bounty land bought by Lt. Col. Hardy Murfree and willed to his daughter and her husband, one of the first practicing doctors in the area. The house has elements of three periods. The original structure, a simple two-story, four-room house, was built around 1815. Modest improvements were made in 1820, and in 1850 it was enlarged to become an elegant antebellum home in the Romanesque Revival style. In December 1862, Jefferson Davis and his aide, Colonel George W. C. Lee, son of Robert E. Lee, stayed at Oaklands while visiting troops in the area. Union Colonel W. W. Duffield commanded the occupation of Murfreesboro from Oaklands, and it was there that he surrendered the town to Confederate General Nathan Bedford Forrest. The home is restored to its 1865 appearance, with furnishings authentic to the period. The site includes a *Medical Museum* housing a small collection of unusual medical implements and artifacts. Open Tues.–Sat. 10–4:30, Sun. 1–4:30. Closed major holidays. Nominal charge; group rates available. 615-893-0022.

NASHVILLE Land speculation was the impetus for many of the early Tennessee settlements, incuding Nashville.

In 1779 Richard Henderson, the ambitious proprietor of the Transylvania Company, found his designs on Kentucky thwarted and turned his attentions to the Cumberland Basin in Tennessee. Henderson, who had a genuine gift for engaging competent frontiersmen to carry out his ventures, commissioned James Robertson—the taciturn Scotch-Irish frontiersman who had been one of the original leaders of the Watauga settlement until he was superseded by John Sevier—to found a settlement in the Cumberland Valley. In the winter of 1779–80, Robertson built Fort Nashborough (see below), and he was soon joined by a party under John Donelson that included his daughter, Rachel Donelson, the future wife of Andrew Jackson.

As a port on the Cumberland River and the northern terminus of the Natchez Trace, Nashville soon became a commercial center of the new west, and in part because of its transportation and communication advantages, it became the state capital in 1843. After the fall of Fort Donelson, the Confederacy abandoned Nashville, in February 1862, and for the rest of the war it was an important staging area for Union efforts in the west.

The *Nashville Tourist Information Center,* 300 Main Street, at I-65 (exit 85) and the James Robertson Parkway, provides tourist information and a room-finder service for travelers. Open daily 9–6 September through May, 9–8 June through August. 615-244-8500.

An enclosed observation deck on the thirty-first floor of the *Life and Casualty Tower,* Fourth Avenue North and Church Street, provides a 30-mile overview of Nashville and its surroundings. Open Mon.–Wed. 8–4:30; Fri.–Sat. 8 A.M.—10:30 P.M.; Sun. noon–6. Nominal charge.

Riverboat cruises on the Cumberland River depart morning and afternoon during the summer from Fort Nashborough, First Avenue North near Broadway. Sight-seeing cruises aboard the 250-passenger sternwheeler, the *Captain Ann,* last 2½ hours. Summer cruises depart at 10:30 and 2:30. Spring and fall cruises are less frequent, and during December, January, and February, cruises are available only by group arrangement. Fare charged. Cruises featuring dinner and entertainment are offered nightly in summer and weekend evenings in spring and fall. Fare charged. The *Nashville Showboat,* docked at Fort Nashborough, is a dinner theater, with performances Thurs.–Sun. June to mid-September. Admission fee charged. Write Belle Carol Riverboat Co., 6043 Charlotte Avenue, Nashville, TN 37209. 615-356-4120.

Gray Line Tours offers ten different tours of Nashville for various fees. 615-244-7330 twenty-four hours.

Despite a disastrous fire in 1916 and a tornado in 1933, several handsome nineteenth-century buildings survive in Nashville. The *First Presbyterian Church* (1849–51), 154 Fifth Avenue, in Egyptian Revival style, has square corner-towers with octagonal belfries and elaborate interior Egyptian styling. The *Federal Office Building,* or customshouse (1875–82), on Broadway, in High Victorian Gothic style with elaborate stone carving and stained-glass work, was built in the effort to rejuvenate the South with Federal money following Reconstruction.

Several historic commercial districts should interest observers of urban architecture. The *Nashville Arcade,* between Fourth and Fifth avenues, inspired by the Galleria in Milan, Italy, is one of only a few remaining late-nineteenth- and early-twentieth-century shopping arcades in the United States. The 378-foot arcade has shops on the first and second floors, connecting bridges, open metal trusses, and a gabled skylighted roof. The *Second Avenue Commercial District,* Second Avenue between Brandon Street and Broadway, is a mid- to late-nineteenth-century commercial streetscape featuring iron ground-floor storefronts.

Music Row, an area of several blocks along Sixteenth Avenue South, is the traditional center of the Nashville music industry and the site of many recording studios and music publishing companies.

Printers' Alley, in downtown Nashville, once the location of three newspaper printing firms, is now the center of Nashville nightlife, lined with restaurants and clubs featuring musical performers for a variety of tastes.

Opryland U.S.A., 9 miles from downtown Nashville, off Briley Parkway, north of I-40, is a family entertainment park emphasizing a wide variety of musical shows. Five musical theme areas ranging from country music to *I Hear America Singing,* a nostalgic review of American popular music, through 1950s rock 'n' roll, to *On with the Show,* a Broadway revue, have continuous live performances. The 110-acre park also includes amusement rides, specialty restaurants, animal exhibits, and craft shows. Hours vary throughout the year. Late March through late May: Sat. 10–8, Sun. 10–6, (weekends only). Late May and early June: Sun.–Fri. 10–6, Sat. 10–8. Early June through late August: daily 10–10. Late August and early September: Mon.–Fri. 10–6, Sat.–Sun. 10–10. Early September through late October: Sat. 10–7, Sun. 10–6 (weekends only). A single admission covers all shows and rides. A special admission ticket for two consecutive days is cheaper. Children under four free. Write the park at Room 101, 2800 Opryland Drive, Nashville, TN 37214. 615-889-6600.

The *"Grand Ole Opry,"* now broadcast from Opryland, is the oldest continuously running radio program in the United States. On November 28, 1925, an octogenarian fiddle-player, Uncle Jimmy Thompson, and a young announcer, George D. Hay, who called himself "The Solemn Old Judge," met in the studios of WSM Radio for the first broadcast of "The WSM Barn Dance." The name "Grand Ole Opry" was coined in the

Ryman Auditorium in Nashville, built originally as a tabernacle for revival meetings, was the home of the "Grand Ole Opry" from 1943 until 1974.

Elvis Presley's 1960 Cadillac, with a 24-karat-gold–plated television set, a gold refreshment bar with gold ice trays, and an engraved gold phone, is one of the favorite exhibits at the Country Music Hall of Fame in Nashville.

late 1920s, and the show has never missed a Saturday-night broadcast in more than half a century. A phenomenally popular stage show, the "Opry" is seen in person by more than 800,000 fans each year.

Two Saturday-night performances, at 6:30 and 9:30, are held year-round. Two Friday-night performances are held in summer; a single Friday show is held at 7:30 in spring and fall. Because performers are scheduled week-to-week, programs are not announced in advance. Nevertheless, reserve tickets, available by mail, are usually sold out weeks in advance. If you can't plan that far ahead, general-admission tickets, which are not sold by mail, are available during the week before the performance. Matinee performances are scheduled for Friday and Saturday afternoons during the peak summer season. These matinee shows are not broadcast but are otherwise similar to the evening performances. For a detailed schedule of performance dates and further ticket information, including an order form, write The Grand Ole Opry Ticket Office, 2808 Opryland Drive, Nashville, TN 37214. 615-889-3060.

Ryman Auditorium (1889–91), 116 Opry Place (Fifth Avenue North), was the home of the "Grand Ole Opry" from 1943 to 1974. This High Victorian Gothic building, built originally as a tabernacle for revivalists, was used in the early 1900s for appearances by less divine entertainers, lecturers, and artists. After outgrowing the studios of WSM Radio, the "Opry" moved to a tabernacle, a theater, the War Memorial Auditorium, and then to Ryman, before arriving at its present home in 1974. Open daily 8:30–4:30. Guided tours daily. Nominal charge. 615-749-1422.

At the *Country Music Hall of Fame,* 4 Music Square East, thirty-three great country musicians are honored by displays in the Central Hall. The museum includes Elvis Presley's "solid gold" Cadillac, a typical touring bus, a Thomas Hart Benton mural, "The Sources of Country Music," folk instruments, dioramas, films, costumes, and a hands-on exhibit of musical instruments. *Studio B,* one block from the museum on Music Row, was once the Nashville headquarters of RCA. Elvis Presley, Chet Atkins, Hank Snow, and others recorded many of the classic country performances here. Visitors are given a guided tour, a review of the studio's history, and a demonstration of modern multitrack recording techniques. A combined admission covers the Hall of Fame, the museum, and Studio B. Open daily 9–5 September through May, 8–8, June through August. Fee charged. Separate admission tickets and group rates are available. Write the Country Music Hall of Fame, 4 Music Square East, Nashville, TN 37203. 615-244-2522.

The *Country Music Wax Museum,* on Music Row, at 116 Sixteenth Avenue South, displays lifelike figures of fifty famous country-music stars. Open daily 9–8 June through August, Mon.–Thurs. 9–5, Fri.–Sat. 9–5:30, Sun. 9–5 September through May. Nominal charge. Group rates available. 615-256-2490.

The *Tennessee State Capitol,* on Capitol Hill, is a Greek Revival capitol modeled after the choragic monument of Lysicrates. It was completed in 1855 and has been the seat of Tennessee government for more than a century. It was the principal commission in the career of architect William Strickland. On the grounds are the tomb of President James K. Polk and statues of Andrew Jackson, Sergeant Alvin York, and Sam Davis, boy hero of the Confederacy. Open Mon.–Fri. 8–4:30, Sat.–Sun. 9:30–4. Free guided tours. 615-741-3211.

The *Governor's Residence,* 822 South Curtiswood Lane, is a stately brick and stone Georgian mansion. Open Tues. and Thurs. 1–3 by appointment. Free. 615-383-5401.

The *Tennessee State Museum* is in the James K. Polk Office Building and Cultural Complex at Fifth Avenue and Deadrick

The Tennessee State Capitol crowns the highest hill in Nashville. Completed in 1855, it was the principal commission in the career of architect William Strickland, who is entombed within its walls.

Street, which also houses state offices, educational television facilities, and a three-theater performing-arts center. The museum displays artifacts representing life in Tennessee from prehistoric times to the present. The museum's military-history branch, which depicts the role of Tennessee in modern wars, is in the War Memorial Building in front of the capitol. Open Mon.–Sat. 10–5, Sun. 1–5; closed holidays. Free. 615-741-2692.

The Upper Room Chapel and Museum, 1908 Grand Avenue, near Vanderbilt University, under the direction of the United Methodist Church, includes in its chapel a 17-foot-wide lime wood and walnut carving of Leonardo's "Last Supper" by Ernest Pelligrini, a stained-glass window depicting Christian history, devotional artifacts from around the world, and a library of 11,000 volumes. The *Agape Garden* represents through symbolism the story of the Christian faith. Open daily 8–4:30 except holidays. Free. 615-327-2700, ext. 444.

The *Belmont Mansion* (1850), Belmont Boulevard, is one of the most splendid of the surviving Southern mansions. The two-story brick and stone Greek Revival house is surrounded by lavish gardens and grounds, with summerhouses, a marble fountain, and a brick water tower that was once part of an extensive irrigation system. For the latter half of the nineteenth-century Belmont was a favorite setting of Nashville social life. Open Fri.–Sat. 10–4. Nominal charge; children free. 615-383-7001.

Traveller's Rest, Farrell Parkway, is the restored home of Judge John Overton, who helped plan the election campaign of his law partner, Andrew Jackson. The eighteenth- and nineteenth-century frame home, L-shaped with a full-length, two-story balustraded porch on the inside of the ell, contains authentic period furnishings. Open Mon.–Sat. 9–4, Sun. 1–4. Closed major holidays. Fee charged. 615-882-2962.

In the midst of contemporary Nashville stands a replica of Fort Nashborough, with re-creations of five log cabins from the late-eighteenth-century settlement overlooking the Cumberland River.

The carriage house of the Belle Meade Mansion in Nashville contains one of the largest collections of horse-drawn vehicles in the South. Belle Meade was once the largest Thoroughbred-breeding farm in America.

The Parthenon in Nashville's Centennial Park, built for the Tennessee Centennial Exposition of 1897, is an exact-size replica of the famous Greek structure. Today it is the focal point of Nashville's city-park system and hosts art exhibitions and craft activities.

The Hermitage, the elegant home built in 1818–19 for Andrew Jackson, is just east of Nashville. On the grounds are the graves of Andrew and Rachel Jackson and the original log cabin in which they lived while the mansion was under construction.

Fort Nashborough, 170 First Avenue North, two blocks north from the foot of Broadway, is a log replica of the original settlement overlooking the Cumberland River. Settlers from the Watauga settlement in eastern Tennessee arrived in two separate parties. An overland trek led by James Robertson arrived in December 1779, and a boat flotilla led by John Donelson arrived in April 1780. Five of the original Nashborough cabins are accurately re-created and complemented by an interpretative program. Open Tues.–Sat. 9–4. Free. 615-255-8192.

The *Belle Meade Mansion* (1853), Harding Road (U.S. 70 South) at Leake Avenue, is the elegant Greek Revival mansion of one of the first Thoroughbred breeding farms in America and, at one time, the largest. The Belle Meade stud, begun in 1835 by W. G. Harding, produced Iroquois, until 1954 the only American-bred winner of the English Derby (1881), Luke Blackburn, and Bonnie Scotland and his son Bramble, founders of the family of Thoroughbreds from which Secretariat is descended. In 1902, the last horses were sold, and two years later, heirs sold the property at auction. On the 24 acres remaining of the once 5,300-acre plantation, stand the mansion itself, the original log cabin where Harding was born, a Tudor-Gothic–style stone dairy house, a gardener's house, the Harding mausoleum, and the large Victorian carriage house and stable that covers nearly an acre and houses a fine collection of carriages from the grand Imperial Park Drag to the humble pony cart. Open Mon.–Sat. 9–5, Sun. 1–5. Final tour begins at 4:30. Closed major holidays. Fee charged. 615-352-7350.

The *Parthenon,* in Centennial Park, entrance at West End Avenue and Twenty-fifth Avenue, is an exact-size duplicate of the Parthenon in Athens, Greece. An earlier frame-and-stucco replica, built for the Tennessee Centennial Exposition of 1897, was razed in 1920 and replaced by the present reinforced concrete building, which is true within $1/16$ inch to the precise dimensions of the original in Athens. Art galleries in the basement have rotating exhibitions and permanent collections, including the Cowan Collection, sixty-three paintings by such American masters of the late nineteenth- and early-twentieth-centuries as Frederick Church and Winslow Homer, a contemporary collection, and a pre-Columbian collection with works from Middle Tennessee and South America. Open Tues.–Sat. 9–4:30, Sun. 1–4:30. Free. 615-327-3413. The *Centennial Arts Center*, also in the park, houses continuous art or craft displays by local and national artists. Open Mon.–Fri. 9–5, Sun. 1–5. Free musical concerts Sunday afternoons during July and August. 615-259-5538.

The *Hermitage* (1818–19), 12 miles east of Nashville on U.S. 70 North, was the home of President Andrew Jackson (1767–1845), who by his personification of the pioneer spirit and his expansion of federal and presidential authority, so powerfully impressed himself upon his era that historians have come to refer to it as the "Age of Jackson." As president, he is remembered for the spoils system of political appointments, which he initiated, and for the brutal relocation of the American Indians to lands west of the Mississippi River. In 1804, Jackson purchased 625 acres, on which stood two log cabins where he and his family lived while he was establishing his reputation as an Indian fighter and soldier with his defeat of the Creeks (1813–14) and his victory over the British at New Orleans (January 8, 1815). The Hermitage mansion, built in 1819, was damaged by fire in 1834 and rebuilt from the original foundations. The entire estate is preserved much as it was at Jackson's death in 1845. The mansion itself is one of the few important historic houses furnished completely with original pieces. Nearly all known personal effects of the Jacksons are in the house or an adjacent museum. The two log cabins remain; Jackson's presidential carriage has been restored, and the garden, designed in 1819, covers more than an acre and contains fifty varieties of plants. Jackson and his wife, Rachel, are buried in a quiet corner of the garden, under hickory trees grown from a parcel of nuts sent to Jackson in 1830.

Across Lebanon Road from the Hermitage is *Tulip Grove* (1836), the Greek Revival mansion built by Rachel Jackson's nephew, Andrew Jackson Donelson, whose wife, Emily, served as hostess of the White House during most of the Jackson administration. The *Hermitage Church* adjacent to Tulip Grove was erected in 1823 by Jackson for his wife. The Hermitage properties are open daily 8–6 June 1 to Labor Day, daily 9–5 the rest of the year. Admission charge covers all properties. 615-889-2941.

Cheekwood, Tennessee Botanical Gardens and Fine Arts Center is on Cheek Road. Cheekwood, built in 1929–32 as the private estate of Mr. and Mrs. Leslie Cheek, was furnished with treasures collected by the owners from many of the great eighteenth-century English mansions. The spiral staircase came from the palace of Queen Charlotte at Kew Gardens in London, the doors from the London home of the Duke of Westminster, and several chandeliers from the home of the Countess of Scarborough. The estate now serves as a regional cultural center. Modern galleries in the sixty-room mansion host showings of private and public art collections. The estate's botanical gardens, greenhouses, streams, forests, and trails are administered by the Botanic Hall on the grounds, which contains a library, laboratory, and exhibition hall for botanical exhibits and serves as a center for research in regional environmental problems. The gardens include beautiful boxwood and tulip plantings, a Japanese sand garden, an orchid greenhouse, an herb and perennial garden, and two sculptured artificial streams. Open Tues.–Sat. 10–5, Sun. 1–5. Closed major holidays. A luncheon is served Tues.–Sat.

11–2. Nominal charge; children under six free with an adult. To get to Cheekwood, take Harding Road to the intersection of Routes 100 and 70. Turn left on Route 100, go ½ mile to Cheek Road, and turn left to the entrance. Two buses leave downtown Nashville daily for Belle Meade and Cheekwood. 615-352-5310.

Vanderbilt University Art Gallery, at Twenty-third and West End avenues, houses the combined collections of recently merged Vanderbilt University and George Peabody College for Teachers, a total of more than two thousand works. Special collections include the Kress Collection of twelve Italian Renaissance paintings, the Hoyt Collection of master prints, and the Stern Collection of Oriental art. The Vanderbilt Fine Arts Building was built in 1880 as a gymnasium, one of the earliest in the South. Gallery open weekdays 1–4, weekends 1–5. Closed university holidays and occasionally in the summer. Free. 615-322-2831.

Jubilee Hall, Seventeenth Avenue North, on the campus of *Fisk University,* is the oldest permanent building for the higher education of blacks in the country. In 1871 the Jubilee Singers, a student chorus, made a successful international tour singing Negro spirituals, and the proceeds paid for the construction of Jubilee Hall.

Fair Park is an amusement park on the Tennessee State Fairgrounds. Open weekends only in May. Open June–September, Mon.–Fri. 2–10, Sat. 10 A.M.–11 P.M., Sun. 1–11. Free admission, charge for rides. 615-256-6494. The *Nashville Speedway,* also on the fairgrounds, hosts NASCAR stock-car racing on a ⅝-mile track. Open Sat. at 8 P.M., April through October. Fee charged for tickets. 615-242-4343.

Cumberland Museum and Science Center, 800 Ridley Avenue, has daily live animal shows and collections of wild creatures displayed in their natural habitats. Planetarium shows, which change every six weeks, are offered on Tuesdays, Saturdays, and Sundays and on Thursday and Friday evenings at 7:30. Exhibits of Indian relics, multimedia sight-and-sound shows, and frequently changing scientific exhibits are other offerings. Open Tues.–Sat. 10–5, Sun. 1–5. Closed holidays. Nominal charge. Free admission on Tuesdays. Additional nominal charge for planetarium shows. 615-242-1858.

Percy Priest and *Old Hickory lakes* offer bass fishing and recreation at various locations around the shores. The *Percy Priest Lake Visitor Center* is open daily 10–4.

The *Tennessee Game Farm and Zoo,* 19 miles northwest off U.S. 41A, is devoted to the propagation of rare and endangered species from all continents. March through November Tues.–Sun. from 9 to 1½ hours before sunset. Open weekends only the rest of the year, or by appointments for groups. Fee charged; under five free. 615-746-5667.

The *Tennessee Agricultural Museum,* Harding Place, is at the Ellington Agricultural Center, the headquarters of the Tennessee Department of Agriculture. Exhibits depict the history of farming as a way of life in Tennessee through displays of hand tools, horse-drawn equipment, household implements, and other early farm articles. *Brentwood Hall,* the administration building, is a replica of the Hermitage; its entrance hall is graced by a circular stairway, French murals, and antique European furnishings. Tours by appointment Mon.–Fri. 8–4:30. Free.

NATCHEZ TRACE PARKWAY This recreational roadway follows the 450-mile path of the frontier road that once extended from Natchez on the Mississippi River northeast to Nashville. Because virtually all the navigable rivers in the lower Mississippi Valley flow in a southerly direction, boatmen who floated farm products from Virginia, Pennsylvania, and Kentucky to the Gulf of Mexico before the age of steamboats had to trudge home overland. Use of the Trace began to grow in the late eighteenth century, while Natchez was still under Spanish dominion. In 1800, the United States created the Mississippi Territory, with Natchez as its capital, and designated the Trace as a post road. After 1803, when New Orleans and the Gulf came permanently under American control, the flow of traffic increased and remained heavy until the advent of steamship traffic on the Mississippi. By 1819 twenty steamboats were navigating up, as well as down, the river, and when the tedious and dangerous return overland was no longer necessary, the Trace soon reverted to a lonely forest path.

Headquarters for the Parkway are at the Tupelo Visitor Center, Rural Route 1, NT-143, Tupelo, MS 38801. 601-842-1572. The following are among the landmarks along the Tennessee segment of the Parkway:

The Parkway crosses into Tennessee from Alabama south of Collinwood. Near its intersection with Route 13, three sections of the original roadway, the *Old Trace,* are discernible.

Sweetwater Branch, farther north, is the site of a nature trail through bottomland forest. A picnic area, *Glenrock,* is accessible by a short trail.

Old Trace Loop Drive, north of U.S. 64, is a 2.5-mile drive along a section of the old Trace, with several scenic overlooks and exhibits portraying the hardships endured by early travelers.

Napier Mine and *Metal Ford* are exhibit areas that demonstrate early iron mining and manufacturing processes.

Meriwether Lewis Park, at Gordonsburg, a campground and picnic area, honors the Virginian who, with his companion, William Clark, explored the Northwest and reached the Pacific Ocean in the autumn of 1805. Lewis was later appointed governor of the Upper Louisiana Territory by his mentor, Thomas Jefferson, but political and financial difficulties soon clouded his life, which ended on the Natchez Trace under suspicious circumstances. Traveling to Washington in 1809 to tidy his affairs, he stopped overnight at Grinder's Stand in Tennessee and was found dead on the roadside the following morning, the victim of either murder or suicide. His grave in the park is marked by a broken column, symbolic of the failed promise of his career. Gordonsburg is the present northern terminus of the Parkway; when completed, the Parkway will extend along the route of the old Trace to Nashville.

PALL MALL   Alvin C. York, recipient of the Congressional Medal of Honor in World War I and described by General John J. Pershing as "the greatest soldier of the war," was born and grew up in the rural settlement of Pall Mall, on Route 28. York, whose initial claim for conscientious-objector status was denied, became a national hero for his actions in the Battle of Argonne Forest on October 8, 1918. The town of Pall Mall is recognized as the *Sergeant Alvin York Historic Area* and includes log and frame homes, a stone Bible school, a chapel, and the York farm and gristmill. Open daily 8–6. Free.

The nearby town of *Jamestown* was for several years the home of John C. Clemens, the father of Mark Twain (Samuel L. Clemens), and is the "Obedstown" of *The Gilded Age* and the location of the "Tennessee land" with which the Hawkins family is so obsessed in the novel. John Clemens himself was apparently obsessed with the value of his own large land grants in Fentress County, for which he designed the first courthouse and county jail, completed in 1827.

READYVILLE   The *Readyville Mill,* on U.S. 70, is perhaps the largest and best preserved nineteenth-century water-powered mill remaining in Tennessee. The original mill, built in 1812 on the East Fork of the Stones River by Charles Ready, burned during the Civil War. Rebuilt after the war, the mill was bought in 1889 by William Haynes, his son Sam, and their partner, William McFerrin, who mechanized and expanded it. Readyville became one of the first rural communities to have electricity when the owners linked an electric generator to the mill in 1902 and offered the service to local residents for about 50 cents a month. In the early twentieth century, the mill operation provided flour, lumber, electricity, and ice to the community. The large timber-framed mill building remains, its five levels surmounted by a gabled roof, and its huge millstones continue to produce stone-ground flour and meal, which is sold at a country store on the premises. The *Charles Ready House (The Corners)*, U.S. 70, once the home of the prominent early settler and builder of the mill, sits astride two counties. The boundary line between Rutherford and Cannon counties passes through the center of the main hall. Private.

ROCK ISLAND *Rock Island State Rustic Park,* on U.S. 70 South, at the upper end of Center Hill Lake, offers picnic and camping sites, a swimming beach, and a boat launch. Write the park at Rock Island, TN 37581. 615-686-2471.

SEWANEE The *University of the South Fine Arts Gallery* houses arts and crafts in many media. Open Mon.–Fri. 10–12 and 2–5, Sat. and Sun. 2–5. Free. 615-518-5917. Arrangements can be made for free guided tours of the campus, which includes Breslin Tower and All Saints Chapel, built after the design of structures at Oxford, England. A 25-foot-high *natural stone bridge* is 4 miles south of Sewanee on Route 56.

SHELBYVILLE Shelbyville, on the Duck River, is named for Colonel Isaac Shelby, who led a force of Tennessee riflemen at Kings Mountain against the American Tories and Loyalists fighting under Major Patrick Ferguson. This is the heart of Tennessee walking-horse country, and in August these magnificent horses with their unique gait are shown at the *National Walking Horse Celebration* at the Celebration Grounds. Write Celebration, Inc., P.O. Box 192, Shelbyville, TN 37160. 615-684-5915. The Shelbyville Chamber of

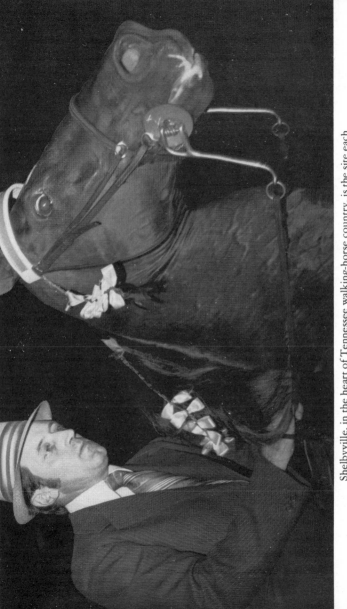

Shelbyville, in the heart of Tennessee walking-horse country, is the site each August of the National Walking Horse Celebration.

Near Smyrna is the home of Sam Davis, executed by the Union as a spy, hailed by the Confederacy as a boy hero. The Davis home is preserved as an example of properous farm life in the Civil War era.

Commerce, 100 North Cannon Boulevard, Shelbyville, TN 37160, phone 615-684-3482, can suggest nearby horse farms and stables that welcome visitors. The *Tennessee Walking Horse Association World Headquarters,* where all registrations, transfers, and decisions concerning the Tennessee walking horses are made, is about 20 miles west of Shelbyville, in Lewisburg.

SHERWOOD *Carter Caves State Natural Area,* on Route 56, encompasses nearly 150 acres including the *Lost Cove Caves.* Picnic areas are available, and a 2-mile trail leads to the caves. Just east of Sherwood is the *Franklin State Forest.*

SILVER POINT *Edgar Evins Rustic State Park,* south of I-40 on Center Hill Lake, is a 6,000-acre park with boating, 60 campsites, and a camp store. Write the park at Silver Point, TN 38582. 615-858-2446.

SMITHVILLE *The Appalachian Center for Crafts,* a professional crafts school associated with Tennessee Technological University in Cookeville, is on a wooded peninsula of Center Hill Lake. The center, which opened in December 1979, is dedicated to preserving and supporting crafts in the Appalachian region and offers professional training in five major media: glass, wood, fiber, metal, and clay. Facilities include a bookstore, crafts store, reference library, and a gallery housing a permanent collection of Appalachian crafts. Write the center at P.O. Box 5106, Tennessee Technological University, Cookeville, TN 38501. 615-597-6801.

SMYRNA The *Sam Davis Home and Museum,* on Route 102 just outside the town, off I-24, was the boyhood home of Sam Davis, who was hanged as a Confederate spy in 1863 after refusing to name his informer in return for a pardon. The two-story clapboard house, which commands a farm of 168 acres on the banks of Stewarts Creek, is of frame and log construction with additional Greek Revival elements, and the original kitchen, smokehouse, overseer's office, and log slave-cabins survive. Many furnishings are those of the Davis family. Behind the house is a formal garden and Sam Davis's grave. Open Mon.–Sat. 9–5, Sun. 1–5 in summer; Mon.–Sat. 10–4, Sun. 1–4 in winter. Nominal charge; group rates available. 615-459-2341.

TULLAHOMA   Visitors are invited to tour the *George Dickel Distillery* on Cascade Road, reached from Tullahoma by taking Alternate 41 North. The George Dickel Collection of antiques and mementos is on display at the nearby general store. Tours Mon.–Fri. 9–3.

WAYNESBORO   Near town, 6 miles northeast, off U.S. 64 (David Crockett Highway), is a *natural bridge,* a pair of twin arches formed by the gradual forces of erosion over millions of years.

WINCHESTER   *Hundred Oaks Castle,* just off U.S. 64, a mile west of the Winchester Square, was built in 1891 by Arthur Handly Marks, son of the twenty-first governor of Tennessee, Albert S. Marks. While serving in the consular service as a young man, Arthur Marks admired the castles he saw in the English and Scottish countryside. When he married and returned home, he built a thirty-seven-room castle of his own, but his enjoyment was short-lived because he died of typhoid fever at age twenty-eight. The castle is now one of the largest antique galleries in the mid-South. Its library is an exact replica of that found in Sir Walter Scott's castle, Abbotsford, in Scotland. Open by appointment. Admission fee charged. 615-967-0100.

The Franklin County *Jail Museum,* on First Avenue in northeast Winchester, houses four rooms of artifacts, documents, photographs, and displays representing the history of Franklin County from pioneer days to the present. Open Thurs.–Sat. 1–5. Donations invited.

Tims Ford State Rustic Park, west of Winchester off Route 130, on Tims Ford Lake, offers boating, fishing, 20 vacation cabins, and 50 developed campsites.

WEST TENNESSEE

West Tennessee, including approximately one-quarter of Tennessee's area, consists of a single physiographic region: the Gulf coastal plain of West Tennessee. Here, in what was once Chickasaw country, the land slopes gently westward in a great plain from the Tennessee River Valley to the Mississippi River. Drained by the Obion, Forked Deer, and Hatchie rivers, among others, this is a rich land of rugged hills and deep alluvial bottomlands. Since before the Civil War, the southern part of West Tennessee has produced cotton and Memphis has been a major cotton market and river port. Because of ties of geography, commerce, and temperament, West Tennesseans have often experienced a kinship with the people of the Deep South, sometimes in conflict with the rest of Tennessee. Reelfoot Lake, in the northern part of West Tennessee, was formed by the New Madrid earthquake of 1811–12. It is the only large natural lake in Tennessee. From Reelfoot, one of the last refuges of the bald eagle, through Shiloh's bloodied ground, to Memphis, Tennessee's largest city, with its history of ancient Indian cultures, paddlewheel steamboats, the blues, jazz, and rock 'n' roll, West Tennessee is a unique region.

BOLIVAR The Hatchie River, by which the farmers of West Tennessee shipped their produce to New Orleans in the nineteenth century, was navigable upstream to Bolivar. The

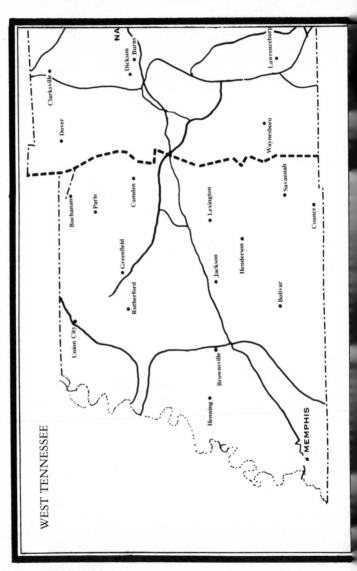

WEST TENNESSEE

Clarksville
Dover
Dickson
Burns
NA
Lawrenceburg
Waynesboro
Buchanan
Paris
Camden
Lexington
Savannah
Counce
Greenfield
Jackson
Henderson
Rutherford
Bolivar
Union City
Brownsville
Henning
MEMPHIS

town, originally called Hatchie, was renamed in 1825 to honor Simon Bolivar (1783–1830), the South American revolutionary leader. The *Little Courthouse,* on East Market Street, built in 1824, was the first courthouse in Hardeman County and remains one of the oldest original courthouses standing in West Tennessee. Converted to a residence in 1849, it is now a property of the Association for the Preservation of Tennessee Antiquities and maintained as a county museum. Open by appointment, inquire locally. Admission charge. Another APTA property, *The Pillars,* the home of John Houston Bills, where Sam Houston and James K. Polk were entertained, is presently undergoing restoration. Write to APTA, Belle Meade Mansion, 110 Leake Avenue, Nashville, TN 37205.

BROWNSVILLE   *Hatchie National Wildlife Refuge* is on the Hatchie River about 10 miles south of Brownsville off Routes 76 and I-40. More than 9,000 acres of timbered bottomland provide shelter for wood ducks, migration and wintering areas for wildfowl, and an excellent habitat for squirrels, raccoons, deer, and turkeys. Hunting and fishing are permitted. Write the refuge at 34 North Lafayette Street, P.O. Box 187, Brownsville, TN 38102.

BUCHANAN   *Paris Landing State Resort Park* is off U.S. 79, on the shores of Kentucky Lake, a 158,300-acre impoundment of the Tennessee River. The park offers a full-service marina, a 100-room inn with dining room, an 18-hole golf course and pro shop, 2 swimming pools, 80 campsites, picnic areas, a camp store, lighted tennis courts, an outdoor game area, and hiking trails. In winter the inn is frequented by duck hunters. Write the park at Buchanan, TN 38222. 901-642-4311.

CAMDEN   *Nathan Bedford Forrest Memorial Park,* 8 miles east of Camden off U.S. 70, overlooks the site where Forrest demolished the Union army supply base at Johnsonville on the Tennessee River in another of his legendary raids.

Forrest, whose simple but classic maxim "get there first with the most" masked a very modern sense of logistics, captured two Union gunboats and used them to harass river traffic and distract attention while he led his horsemen and artillery unnoticed into position on the west bank opposite Johnsonville. On November 4, 1864, at precisely two o'clock—with timepieces carefully synchronized—the Confederate batteries opened on the unsuspecting Union base. Their fire destroyed gunboats, transports, barges, wharves, and a warehouse full of whiskey barrels. Forrest, who suffered only eleven casualties, estimated the Union loss at $6,700,000. Forrest himself embodied at once some of the most and the least admirable qualities of any Confederate officer. From a background of poverty, with little formal education, he had prospered. An intuitively brilliant military tactician, he was respected for his personal courage; his charge at Fallen Timbers was an act of astonishing temerity. However, before the war, Forrest had been a Memphis slave trader, and after the war he became a leader of the Ku Klux Klan. From the park at Pilot Knob, the highest spot in West Tennessee, the Tennessee River is visible for a great distance. Open daily 6–6. Free. Write the park at Eva, TN 38333. 901-584-6356.

COUNCE *Pickwick Landing State Resort Park* is off Route 57, on Pickwick Lake of the Tennessee River. It has a resort inn and restaurant, cabins, a full-service marina, 50 campsites, picnic area, and an 18-hole golf course with pro shop. Write the park at Pickwick Dam, TN 38365. 901-689-3135.

GREENFIELD *Big Cypress Tree State Natural Area,* on U.S. 45E, is a new state nature preserve centered around a giant 18-foot cypress tree, one of many that once covered the surrounding bottomland. An interpretative center, a support facility, and a wooden walkway are planned in this bottomland hardwood forest in the flood plain of the Middle Fork of the Obion River. Write the area at Kimery Road, Greenfield, TN 38230. 901-235-2700.

HENDERSON *Chickasaw Rustic State Park,* off Route 100 southwest of Henderson, includes 11,215 acres in the Chickasaw State Forest and offers 2 lakes, 12 air-conditioned cabins, 75 campsites, a restaurant, and recreation facilities. Write the park at Henderson, TN 38340. 901-989-5141.

HENNING *Fort Pillow State Historic Area,* off Route 87, is a 1,646-acre park located on the site of Fort Pillow, a horseshoe-shaped earthen fort built at the confluence of Cold Creek and the Mississippi River by the Confederate army in 1861. When the Union forces that held the fort 1862–64 surrendered it to a Confederate force under Nathan Bedford Forrest on April 12, 1864, the high proportion of Union casualties suggested the possibility, still disputed, that some might have been incurred after the surrender. Elements of the earthworks remain, and there is a visitor center. Write to Fort Pillow State Historic Area, Box 73, Henning, TN 38041. 901-738-5466.

JACKSON Settled by migrants from North Carolina about 1819 and named for Andrew Jackson, this town was a major railroad center during the nineteenth century. The *Casey Jones Home and Railroad Museum* is at 211 West Chester Street, in downtown Jackson. John Luther Jones, born in 1863, acquired his nickname from his early hometown of Cayce, Kentucky. In 1888, he went to work for the Illinois Central Railroad as a fireman and two years later became an engineer. While living in Jackson, Casey Jones needed extra money, so he substituted for an ailing engineer on a run from Memphis to New Orleans. On April 30, 1900, at the throttle of "Old 382," he met his death near Vaughan, Mississippi, the only casualty of a collision he tried valiantly to prevent. He is buried in Mount Calvary Cemetery on Hardee Street. A black engine wiper in the roundhouse at Canton, Mississippi,

Wallace Saunders, composed the words to the popular ballad "Casey Jones." The home is now a railroad museum, with pictures and memorabilia from the age of steam railroads. An engine of the type in which Jones died is displayed. Open daily 8–8 April 15 through September 15, 9–5 in winter. Nominal charge. 901-668-1222.

The *Brooks Shaw and Son Old Country Store,* Casey Jones Village, 514 Airways Boulevard, is a restaurant furnished with thousands of antiques and fixtures collected from turn-of-the-century country stores. 901-668-1223.

The *Pinson Mounds,* off U.S. 45 southeast of Jackson, on the Forked Deer River, 3 miles east of Pinson on a secondary road, are the remains of a prehistoric Indian civilization from the Woodland–Early Mississippian periods (300 B.C.–A.D. 1000). Within the 1,000-acre site are more than thirty mounds, including flattopped pyramidal temple mounds, a bird-shaped effigy mound, conical burial mounds, and an extensive system of surrounding earthworks. Excavated in 1963 by the University of Tennessee, the site is now used as a tree nursery by the Tennessee Division of Forestry and may be developed as a state park.

The *M. D. Anderson Planetarium* at Lambuth College can realistically portray stars down to fifth magnitude on the 30-foot dome. Admission charge.

LEXINGTON *Natchez Trace State Resort Park and Forest,* the largest park in the Tennessee system, is northeast of Lexington on I-40, about 15 miles west of the Tennessee River. It is named for the eighteenth- and nineteenth-century trail from Natchez to Nashville (see NATCHEZ TRACE PARKWAY), which actually passed many miles to the east. This 43,000-acre park includes four lakes, a twenty-unit resort inn and restaurant complex, cabins, a group lodge, and recreational facilities. Write the park at Wildersville, TN 38388. 615-968-3742.

The Casey Jones Home and Railroad Museum at Jackson preserves the memory of the Illinois Central engineer whose death in a collision in 1900 became the subject of one of the most enduring ballads in American folklore.

The "Big Pecan," one of the largest pecan trees in the world, flourishes in Natchez Trace State Resort Park and Forest in southwestern Tennessee, near Lexington. According to legend, the tree, which is 118 feet tall and has a circumference near its base of more than 18 feet, was planted by one of General Andrew Jackson's men after returning from the Battle of New Orleans.

MEMPHIS   The Chickasaw Indians, who had clung tenaciously to their domain in West Tennessee through the centuries of colonial competition among the French, Spanish, and English, in 1818 ceded to the United States their lands east of the Mississippi. Andrew Jackson, who negotiated the arrangement as an agent of the government, secured in the process a parcel of land on the Mississippi River for himself and his partners, John Overton and James Winchester. Recognizing the advantages of the site—the commanding bluffs and the excellent landing at the mouth of the Wolf River—they laid out lots and planned the city that would become Memphis. Although criticism of their land speculation persuaded Jackson, who by then was more absorbed by political ambition, to sell out his interest, the settlement grew rapidly. Memphis was incorporated in 1826, and by the mid-1830s had assumed the character of a river boomtown. In 1834, the first steamboat line from Memphis to New Orleans began service; in 1850, Memphis became a port of customs. When Memphis was connected to the Atlantic coast by rail in 1857, it became also a center of railroad commerce. As trade and travel flourished, the city burgeoned. The population multiplied more than five times in the 1850s.

The prosperous side of this growth can still be seen in the restored homes and churches of the *Victorian Village District,* a downtown residential area encompassing Adams, Jefferson, and Poplar avenues, which includes a number of well-preserved dwellings from the second half of the nineteenth century in building styles ranging from Neo-classical through Late Gothic Revival and including Federal, Italian Villa, and Queen Anne designs. A similar variety of architecture is evident in nine churches built between 1843 and 1898. Eighteen structures on twelve separate sites will eventually be open daily to the public.

The *Fontaine House,* at 680 Adams Avenue in the Victorian Village District, was built in 1870 for Amos Woodruff, a native of New Jersey who came to Memphis in 1845 and was a founder of the Memphis and Charleston Railroad. The house, named for a later owner, Noland Fontaine, is of elegant, sophisticated Second Empire design. Now restored, it is furnished with Louis XVI, Chippendale, Sheraton, and Queen Anne antiques, Aubusson and Oriental rugs, Carrarra marble mantels, and crystal chandeliers. Open daily 1–4. Other hours by appointment. Nominal charge. 615-526-1469.

The *Mallory-Neely House,* at 652 Adams Avenue in the Victorian Village District, a twenty-five-room mansion with a five-story tower, was built sometime between 1849 and 1861 of stucco over brick. The house and furnishings are now restored to their appearance in the 1890s when James Neely, a prosperous cotton factor and the third owner, enlarged and restyled the house, adding a third floor with dormers, gables, and extended towers. The style is Italian Villa. Open daily 1–4, by appointment 10–1. Nominal charge. 901-527-7965.

The *Magevney House (ca.* 1836), 198 Adams Street, is one of the oldest houses in Memphis, a modest clapboard cottage purchased in 1837 by Eugene Magevney, an Irish immigrant teacher and a founder of the Roman Catholic community in Memphis. In 1839, the first Catholic mass in Memphis was said here. The house is furnished with some of the original family possessions, including portraits, a leather trunk brought from Ireland by Mrs. Magevney, and the desk chair from Eugene Magevney's classroom. Some of the original china doorknobs, plank flooring, and the original door nameplate remain. The grounds include a kitchen garden, grape arbor, and flower garden. Open Tues.–Sat. 10–4, Sun. 1–4. Free.

The section of Beale Street (actually an east-west avenue) from Main to Fourth streets is designated the *Beale Street Historic District.* At the turn of the century, these few blocks,

The Fontaine House, three stories tall, with a view of the Mississippi River from its cupola, is an outstanding example of nineteenth-century French Victorian architecture and a showpiece of the Victorian Village Historic District

lined with saloons, nightclubs, gambling halls, theaters, and pawnshops, were the center of gambling, entertainment, and general lowlife in Memphis. Here were the Palace, Daisy, and Orpheum (still standing) theaters, the Hole-in-the-Wall Saloon, and Peewee's Saloon. *W. C. Handy Park,* at the corner of Beale and Third streets, honors William Christopher Handy. Handy was not, as he is sometimes casually described, the "originator" of the blues; he was, however, an articulate and aware musician who, before 1917, published "Memphis Blues," "Beale St. Blues," and "St. Louis Blues," crystallizations of the folk blues tradition that popularized the name and the twelve-bar form. His statue overlooks the park. The musical heritage of Memphis is perpetuated each May with blues and jazz at the Beale Street Music Festival.

The Mississippi River, "father of waters," is showcased in every aspect at *Mud Island,* an actual island in this greatest of American rivers. Scheduled to open in July 1982 in downtown Memphis, Mud Island is a 50-acre, $60 million entertainment and educational complex devoted to the presentation of the river, its ecology, history, and role as the great artery of American settlement and commerce. Visitors will travel from the riverbank to Mud Island via their choice of a ⅓-mile-long suspended Swiss monorail, a riverboat, or a covered overhead walkway. The monorail will dock at the *River Center,* which houses a restaurant, a theater, and shops. The *River Museum,* in the River Center, preserves and interprets the river's cultural and natural history, folklore, geography, biology, and hydrology in 25,000 square feet of exhibit space. Exhibits will include: prehistoric peoples of the Mississippi Valley; early settlers; scale models of the various boats to ply the river; levees, channels, and bridges; colorful characters of the river's past; Civil War battles; natural and engineering sciences used to harness and protect the river; and the art and music inspired by the river. Highlights include an authentic reconstruction of the front third of an 1870s riverboat, which stands three stories high, is surrounded by water, and includes the grand salon, pilot house, and main deck. A film shown in a reconstruction of the pilot house of a modern towboat simulates the river from the pilot's perspective. A realistic audio program brings to life a full-size reconstruction of the front quarter of a Union gunboat overlooked by a Confederate shore battery. Also on display are an operating riverboat steam engine with turning paddle wheel, an 8-ton diesel towboat engine, and a 4,000-gallon freshwater aquarium. Flowing the length of Mud Island is the *River Walk,* a five-block-long scale model of the lower Mississippi River from Cairo, Illinois, to the Gulf of Mexico. Each 30 inches of the 2,000-foot model represents a mile of river and its configuration is exact even to the water level, which will be regulated each day to match the actual level of the river. Major towns and cities are depicted by proportional mosaics—Memphis is depicted in 144 square feet. Near the south tip of the island, the river model flows into a 3-foot-deep, 1-acre replica of the Gulf of Mexico, from which powerful pumps return the water to the river's source in a closed system that contains more than 1.2 million gallons of water. Other attractions of Mud Island include picnic, playground, and recreation areas, a marina, and lookout points, one of which will have radios tuned to talk among actual river traffic. Mud Island will be open all year: daily in spring, summer, and fall, and on a more limited schedule in winter.

The *Center for Southern Folklore,* 1216 Peabody Avenue, is dedicated to the preservation and appreciation of Southern folk culture. It documents this vanishing culture on film and tape, and its publications serve as a clearinghouse of information about other folklore and media projects. Although primarily a research organization, the center welcomes visitors. Write it at Box 4081, Memphis, TN 38104. 901-726-4205.

The *Memphis Pink Palace Museum and Planetarium,* 3050 Central Avenue, explores the natural and cultural world of the mid-South region, past and present. The Pink Palace, the original home of the museum, is a palatial, pink marble structure begun in the 1920s by Memphis supermarket tycoon Clarence Saunders as his private home. When financial reverses forced him to halt construction, the city acquired the curious unfinished building and opened it as a museum of natural history in 1930. In 1977, the exhibits were moved to an adjacent new facility, and the Pink Palace itself now serves as the educational and administrative wing. The new building houses two floors of exhibits. Natural-history exhibits on the first floor include birds, trees, insects, earthquakes, a huge mosasaur skeleton, geological specimens, and an outdoor re-creation of an oxbow lake. The cultural history of the region is traced by the themes of exhibits on the second floor: cotton, farming, the Civil War, the Clyde Park miniature circus, Memphis 1830–80, and a drugstore re-created as it would have looked at the turn of the century. Temporary exhibits, usually from the Traveling Exhibition Service of the Smithsonian Institution, change about every six weeks. Open Tues.–Thurs. 9–5, Fri. and Sat. 9 A.M.–10 P.M., Sun. 1–6. Closed major holidays. Nominal charge; children under six free. Admission is free Sat. 9–10 A.M. Tours of the original Pink Palace building are provided at no extra charge 1:30–5 on the third Sunday of each month. Group rates by reservation. 901-454-5600.

The planetarium presents scheduled shows, which change periodically, Friday evening, Saturday afternoon and evening, and Sunday afternoon. When school is not in session, additional shows are presented morning and afternoon, Tues.–Fri. Children under six are admitted only to the 4:30 Saturday performance. Nominal charge; senior citizens' discounts; reduced group rates arranged. 901-454-5603.

The Pink Palace, built in the 1920s in Memphis by Clarence Saunders, the originator of the modern concept of the supermarket, now serves as a wing of the Pink Palace Museum.

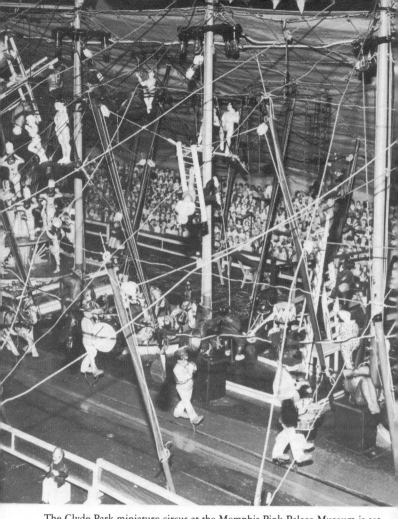

The Clyde Park miniature circus at the Memphis Pink Palace Museum is set in motion on Saturdays and Sundays.

The *Dixon Gallery and Gardens,* 4339 Park Avenue, has galleries housed in a home furnished with English antiques. The galleries include works representing the major art movements of the past three centuries. Although the permanent collection is devoted primarily to works by French and American Impressionists and related schools, there are also eighteenth- and nineteenth-century British portraits and landscapes, and sculpture by British and French artists. Among the artists represented are Cassatt, Chagall, Corot, Degas, Gainsborough, Gauguin, Guillaumin, Matisse, Monet, Renoir, Signac, and Turner. The decorative arts collection includes Sheffield silver, Waterford crystal, Chinese porcelain of the Ch'ien Lung period, and Sèvres porcelain. The 17-acre gardens are reminiscent of the great English landscape parks and include a series of three terraced formal gardens and a circular reflection pool. Open Tues.–Sat. 11–5, Sun. 1–5. Closed major holidays. Nominal charge; group rates available. 901-761-5250.

Overton Park, named for John Overton, one of the founders of Memphis, includes the Memphis Zoological Garden and Aquarium, with thousands of living creatures, exotic and familiar, and a petting zoo for children. Open daily 9–6 in summer, 9–5 in winter. Closed major holidays. Nominal charge for admission; free Sat. 9–10 A.M. 901-725-4768. The *Brooks Memorial Art Gallery,* in Overton Park, houses the Kress Collection of Italian Renaissance art, Flemish and Dutch paintings, French Impressionist works, and American art. Doughty birds highlight the fine porcelain collection. There is also a new gallery for children and special monthly exhibits. Open Tues.–Sat. 10–5, Sun. 1–5. Closed some holidays. 901-726-5266. The *Memphis Academy of Arts,* also in Overton Park, displays the work of students and professionals in its main hall. Open Mon.–Fri. 9–5. Free. 901-726-4085.

Overton Square is a midtown cluster of quaint shops, restaurants, sidewalk cafes, and galleries. The *Playhouse on the Square,* a professional theater, presents summer and fall performance seasons. 901-726-4656.

One third of the annual American cotton crop is bought and sold by members of the Memphis Cotton Exchange, at the corner of Front Street and Union Avenue. Individual and group tours by appointment. Free. Although tobacco and soybeans are now bigger Tennessee crops, Memphis is still the world's largest spot cotton market and still celebrates "King Cotton" each May with the Memphis Cotton Carnival. The *Shelby Cotton Company,* South Front Street, is a working firm, but it welcomes visitors by appointment.

The 88-acre *Memphis Botanical Garden,* 760 Cherry Road in Audubon Park, includes thousands of species of flora, featuring rose and iris gardens, magnolias, and wildflowers. Open Mon.–Fri. 2–5, Sun. dawn to dusk. Free. 901-685-1566.

Libertyland, at the Fairgrounds, East Parkway between Coliseum and Central Avenue, is a theme park with family amusements—music, shops, restaurants, and rides, in settings of historical fantasy, including Colonial Land, Turn-of-the-Century Land, and Frontier Land. Open late May through early September: weekends only in spring, daily from June through Labor Day. All-day admission fee charged; children under six free. 901-274-8800.

Lakeland Amusement Park, east of Memphis on I-40, offers camping, picnicking, fishing, and swimming. Open weekends in May, daily in summer. Nominal admission charge; children under six free.

Graceland, the home of Elvis Presley, 3764 Elvis Presley Boulevard (U.S. 51 South), is closed to the public, but pursuers after the legend are welcome to visit the Meditation Garden, in which are buried Presley and his parents, and to photograph the grounds and mansion.

The Memphis Zoo, which began in 1901 with a black bear cub tied to a tree in Overton Park, is now the 36-acre Memphis Zoological Garden and Aquarium, housing more than 400 species of animals.

Originating in 1912 with a $100,000 donation from the estate of a Memphis grocer, the Brooks Memorial Art Gallery in Overton Park has become one of the oldest and most prominent galleries in the South.

Visitors to Memphis are welcome to visit the graves of Elvis Presley and his parents in the Meditation Garden at Graceland, his mansion.

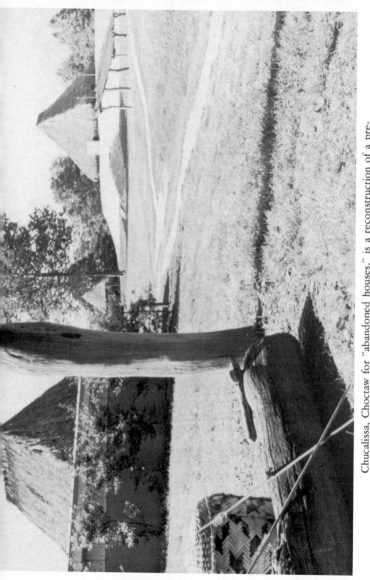

Chucalissa, Choctaw for "abandoned houses," is a reconstruction of a pre-Columbian Indian village within T. O. Fuller State Park at Memphis.

The *Sun Recording Studio,* at Marshall and Union Streets, was one of the birthplaces of rock 'n' roll. There, in the mid-1950s, a new sound in American popular music was forged from elements of country and western, gospel, and rhythm and blues by such pioneers of rock 'n' roll as Elvis Presley, Johnny Cash, B. B. King, Jerry Lee Lewis, Charlie Rich, Carl Perkins, and Roy Orbison. The studios have been restored to their appearance in that period, with vintage instruments, promotional photographs, and original Sun labels. Open daily 8–5, with tours every half hour.

Chucalissa Indian Village and Museum, on Indian Drive, via U.S. 61 South and Mitchell Road west, is on the site of an Indian town founded around A.D. 900 and evidently occupied until the early 1600s. It is one of a small galaxy of Indian communities strung along the eastern shore of the Mississippi River from present-day Memphis south into northern Mississippi. They were deserted sometime between the passage of De Soto in 1541 and the first French explorations of the river in 1673. Based on archeological data, the central mound, plaza, and village complex, including nine surrounding houses, have been reconstructed. An excavation site and museum display recovered artifacts, and Choctaw Indian guides demonstrate how these people might have lived. Open Tues.–Sat. 9–5, Sun. 1–5. Admission to the museum is free; nominal admission charge to the restored village; children under six free. 901-785-3160. *T. O. Fuller State Park,* which includes Chucalissa, also includes 30 campsites, a golf course, a swimming pool, and other recreational facilities. Write the park at 3269 Boxtown Road, Memphis, TN 38109. 901-785-3950.

Meeman-Shelby Forest State Park, 12 miles north of Memphis off U.S. 51, is a large park along a gentle curve of the Mississippi River. It encompasses two lakes, many miles of hiking and bridle trails, a swimming pool, 50 campsites, cabins, a group camp, and the *Meeman Museum and Nature Center.*

The racing season at *Southland Greyhound Park,* just across the river in West Memphis, Arkansas, at I-55 and Ingram Boulevard, runs from mid-May through mid-October. The park has an enclosed grandstand and parimutuel betting. Open daily except Wed. and Sun. Post time 8 P.M.; matinees at 1:30 P.M. Sat. and holidays. Nominal admission charged. 501-735-3670.

The boat-racing season lasts from May through October at *Kilowatt Marine Stadium,* 1900 Chelsea. Events include speed and drag boat-racing and other aquatic events. 901-327-6121.

Memphis *theaters* include the *Circuit Playhouse,* 1947 Poplar, phone 901-726-5521, and the *Playhouse on the Square,* 2121 Madison, phone 901-725-0776. Plant tours of the *Joseph Schlitz Brewing Co.,* 5151 East Raines Road, include the *Schlitz Belle,* a replica of a Mississippi River sternwheeler, and samples of the Schlitz product. Tours Mon.–Fri. 10:30–3:30. Free. 901-362-5450.

The *Memphis Queen Line* offers ninety-minute excursions on the Mississippi River, departing from the foot of Monroe Street and Riverside Street, June through August, Mon.–Fri. 9:30, 2:30, 6:30; Sat. 9:30, 2:30, 4:30, 6:30; Sun. 2:30, 4:30, 6:30. The schedule is reduced in fall, winter, and spring. Fee charged; children under four free. 901-527-5694.

Several commercial tour services offer daily sight-seeing tours of Memphis, often with free pickup at most lodgings. For information on these and other services to visitors, as well as on special events, contact the Convention and Visitors Bureau of Memphis, 12 South Main Street, Suite 107, Memphis, TN 38103, phone 901-526-1919; or the Memphis Area Chamber of Commerce, 42 South Second Street, P.O. Box 224, Memphis, TN 38103, phone 901-523-2322.

PARIS *Tennessee National Wildlife Refuge* is a 51,347-acre wintering area for thousands of waterfowl attracted by a farming program that provides supplemental winter food.

Fishing and hunting are permitted. Write the refuge at Box 849, Paris, TN 38242.

RUTHERFORD The *Crockett Cabin,* on U.S. 45W, is a reproduction of the cabin built by Davy Crockett when he moved to West Tennessee in 1823 and settled on the Rutherford Fork of the Obion River. The original cabin, built about 5 miles east of Rutherford, was intended to have been reassembled here. It was dismantled, and the logs were stored on the local school's grounds; but a traveling carnival camped on the lot one rainy night and used the dry logs to fuel a bonfire. Another cabin of the same era and construction was found, and from it an exact replica of the Crockett cabin was created. The cabin contains furniture, tools, and household utensils of the nineteenth century, as well as letters written by Crockett while he was a congressman from this district. His mother is buried on the grounds. Open daily 9–5 May 1 through Labor Day. Nominal charge. No phone.

SAVANNAH *Shiloh National Military Park and Cemetery* is 12 miles from Savannah via U.S. 64 and Route 22. In the two days of savage fighting that began at Shiloh Church on April 6, 1862, the illusion of easy victory, held by both North and South, was shattered. During the Union march to Corinth, Mississippi, General Ulysses S. Grant, flushed with his easy capture of Forts Henry and Donelson, believed the Confederate army to be "heartily tired," and predicted, "Corinth will fall much more easily." Confederate General Albert Sidney Johnston, advancing northward out of Mississippi, promised his troops that they would water their horses that night in the Tennessee River. Two days later, more than 8,000 men from each army were dead, including Johnston, considered by Jefferson Davis to be the finest soldier alive, and the tenacity of both sides was no longer in question. After Shiloh, Grant said later, "I gave up all idea of saving the Union except by complete conquest." About 100,000 soldiers fought at Shiloh, and approximately one of every four was killed, wounded, or captured. The casualties at Shiloh slightly exceeded the total American casualties from the nation's three preceding wars—the Revolution, the War of 1812, and the Mexican War. And Shiloh was only the beginning, the first major land encounter in the contest for the Mississippi Valley. *Shiloh National Military Park,* established in 1894, includes the battlefield with a 9-mile self-guided automobile tour, monuments erected to the dead of both sides, a library and museum with relics and maps, and a visitors' center where a twenty-five-minute movie describes the battle. The grounds never close. The visitor center is open daily 8–6 Memorial Day to Labor Day, 8–5 the rest of the year. Free. 901-689-5275.

TIPTONVILLE   *Reelfoot Lake State Resort Park* is off Route 21 east of Tiptonville. In 1811 and 1812, a series of violent earthquakes disrupted western Tennessee, creating Reelfoot Lake where a dense forest once stood. The partially submerged trees created a fertile fish hatchery, and fishermen, hunters, and trappers frequented its shores. In his autobiography (which he may or may not have written himself), Davy Crockett describes his bear-hunting days at Reelfoot Lake in the early nineteenth century. In 1908 two promoters who planned to develop the lake were attacked by Reelfoot fishermen; one escaped, the other was lynched. Today, the state park is one of Tennessee's most scenic. A resort inn and restaurant are built out over the water's edge among the cypress trees, and there are vacation cabins, scenic cruise boats, a recreation hall, seventy-five developed campsites, a camp store, a museum, and an auditorium. Reelfoot Lake, almost 20 miles long, is a favorite wintering area for bald eagles. Commercial fishing is permitted, and the rough fish discarded by the fishermen are the preferred diet of bald eagles. Bus tours daily December 1 through March 15, and visitors are

The partially submerged forest of Reelfoot Lake is a productive fish hatchery. The 14,500-acre lake, created by earthquakes in 1811 and 1812, is now the heart of Reelfoot Lake State Resort Park near Tiptonville.

The distinctive white-capped head of a mature bald eagle, dozens of which spend January and February at Reelfoot Lake, living off the leavings of commercial fishermen while they wait for their northern habitats to thaw. Guided tours at Reelfoot Lake State Resort Park, east of Tiptonville, offer an excellent opportunity to observe these magnificent raptors.

encouraged to join a tour rather than pursue the birds on their own. The tours are free, but reservations are required. Write the Superintendent, Reelfoot Lake State Park, Tiptonville, TN 38079. 901-253-7756.

Reelfoot National Wildlife Refuge, with headquarters in Samburg, east of Tiptonville via Routes 21 and 22, includes some 11,000 acres of the Reelfoot Lake area. The smaller *Lake Isom National Wildlife Refuge,* 5 miles south, is also administered by Reelfoot Refuge. Both areas serve primarily as refuges for wintering ducks and geese, but more than 240 species of fowl find a haven there. Write the refuge at Box 295, Samburg, TN 38254. 901-538-2481.

UNION CITY   The Dixie Gun Works, on U.S. 51 bypass, is perhaps the most widely known dealer of antique guns and manufacturer of replicas in the world. The personal collection of founder Turner Kirkland, which began with a Colt 1894 pocket-model percussion revolver acquired at the age of twelve in 1932, has become an inventory of around 1,500 antique revolvers and rifles, most made before 1898. Hundreds of these old weapons are displayed in the Dixie Gun Works' headquarters, a virtual museum of early gunsmithing and manufacturing, with thousands of gun parts, bullet molds, powder horns, and other accoutrements. Most of these antique guns are for sale, along with the black-powder muzzle-loading replicas manufactured by the Dixie Gun Works. On the same site the *Old Car Museum* displays thirty-one antique automobiles, all restored and in running order, including a 1908 Maxwell, a 1910 Waverly Electric, and a 1912 Cadillac. Open Mon.–Fri. 8–5, Sat. 8–12. Nominal charge. 901-885-0700.

Turner Kirkland, founder and proprietor of the Dixie Gun Works at Union City, displays one of his favorite antique guns, a Kentucky long rifle made in North Carolina in the 1820s.

4302-10-SB
5-26
C

GEOGRAPHIC INDEX